eSERVICE-LEARNING

eSERVICE-LEARNING

Creating Experiential Learning and Civic Engagement Through Online and Hybrid Courses

EDITED BY

Jean Strait and Katherine J. Nordyke

Foreword by
Andrew Furco

STERLING, VIRGINIA

Sty/us

Published by Stylus Publishing, LLC
22883 Quicksilver Drive
Sterling, Virginia 20166-2102

Library of Congress Cataloging-in-Publication Data
eService-learning : creating experiential learning and civic engagement
through online and hybrid courses / edited by Jean R. Strait and
Katherine Nordyke ; foreword by Andrew Furco. -- First edition.
    pages cm
Includes bibliographical references and index.
ISBN 978-1-62036-063-7 (cloth : alk. paper)
ISBN 978-1-62036-064-4 (pbk. : alk. paper)
ISBN 978-1-62036-065-1 (library networkable e-edition)
ISBN 978-1-62036-066-8 (consumer e-edition)
1. Service learning–Technological innovations. 2. Service learning–
Study and teaching (Higher) 3. Internet in higher education. I.
Strait, Jean, 1965- editor of compilation. II. Nordyke, Katherine,
editor of compilation.
LC220.5.E74 2015
378.1'03–dc23
                                                                2014042531
13-digit ISBN: 978-1-62036-063-7 (cloth)
13-digit ISBN: 978-1-62036-064-4 (paperback)
13-digit ISBN: 978-1-62036-065-1 (library networkable e-edition)
13-digit ISBN: 978-1-62036-066-8 (consumer e-edition)

Printed in the United States of America

All first editions printed on acid-free paper
that meets the American National Standards Institute
Z39-48 Standard.

First Edition, 2015

10   9   8   7   6   5   4   3   2   1

Katherine
I would like to dedicate this book in honor of my family, Gary, Kami, David, JJ, Kristina, Samantha, Austin, Andrew, Ashton, Kyleigh, Garrison, and Jackson; in memory of my parents and grandfather, Jean and Chuck Andrews and C. H. Irvin; and my husband's parents, Rex and Vada Nordyke.

Jean
I would like to dedicate this book to my son, Kyle Clinton Kermit Alexander; I love you more than anything on this planet! I am your nerd, and don't you forget it. We are never really far apart—our hearts are always together.

CONTENTS

FOREWORD   ix
Andrew Furco

ACKNOWLEDGMENTS   xiii

INTRODUCTION   1

**PART ONE: ESSENTIALS, COMPONENTS, AND NUTS AND
BOLTS OF eSERVICE-LEARNING**

1. PEDAGOGY OF CIVIC ENGAGEMENT, HIGH-IMPACT
   PRACTICES, AND eSERVICE-LEARNING   7
   Jean Strait, Jane Turk, and Katherine J. Nordyke

2. eSERVICE-LEARNING   20
   Breaking Through the Barrier
   Leora Waldner

3. DEVELOPING AN eSERVICE-LEARNING EXPERIENCE FOR
   ONLINE COURSES   40
   Katherine J. Nordyke

4. SUPPORTING eSERVICE-LEARNING THROUGH TECHNOLOGY   58
   Jean Strait

PART TWO: MODELS FOR eSERVICE-LEARNING

5. HYBRID I
   Missouri State University Embraces eService-Learning   69
   Katherine J. Nordyke

6. HYBRID II
   A Model Design for Web Development   89
   Pauline Mosley

7. HYBRID III: EACH ONE, TEACH ONE   105
    Lessons From the Storm
        Jean Strait

8. HYBRID IV: EXTREME eSERVICE-LEARNING   119
    Online Service-Learning in an Online Business Course
        Sue McGorry

9. MIXED HYBRID: HYBRID I AND HYBRID III
    eSERVICE-LEARNING   130
    Investigating the Influence of Online Components on
    Service-Learning Outcomes at the University of Georgia
        Paul H. Matthews

PART THREE: NEXT STEPS AND FUTURE DIRECTIONS

10. COMMUNITY ENGAGEMENT AND TECHNOLOGY FOR A
    MORE RELEVANT HIGHER EDUCATION   149
        John Hamerlinck

11. CONCLUSIONS, RECOMMENDATIONS, AND FINAL THOUGHTS   164
        Jean Strait

    EDITORS AND CONTRIBUTORS   167

    INDEX   173

Two fast-growing contemporary educational practices that are changing the face of classroom instruction are online learning and service-learning. Each practice has gained a global following among educators, establishing a track record of turning dismissive skeptics into strong advocates. With growing prominence, each practice has built a literature and research base that demonstrates its potential for enhancing student learning and success. While these instructional approaches have, for the most part, operated in parallel, we are now witnessing a growing interest among educators in linking these two modes of instruction.

Linking of online learning (or e-learning) and service-learning has spawned a hybrid practice known as electronic-service-learning or eService-Learning. As described in this volume, eService-Learning blends the best features of service-learning and online learning to create educational experiences that neither practice can produce alone. What might at first glance seem like an unlikely pairing—online, virtual learning linked with hands-on, community-engaged, experiential learning—eService-Learning serves as a vehicle for extending the reach and impact of students' service-learning experiences, while ensuring that online learning activities are relevant, contextualized, and linked to civic responsibility. To online learning, eService-Learning has the potential to bring authenticity and relevance to students' virtual understanding of situations by engaging students in real-life, real-time, community-situated service-learning experiences. To service-learning, eService-Learning has the potential to deepen and broaden the impact of students' community-based experiences by incorporating online activities that can extend the reach of students' work beyond their local communities. By blending the virtual with the real, and the on-site with the online, eService-Learning is capitalizing on today's students' love of technology and their generational propensities to engage with and contribute to society.

As the chapters in this volume detail, the proliferation of rapidly advancing technologies has substantially raised the profile of online education in academia. Indeed, massive open online courses (MOOCs), blended learning (in-class instruction coupled with online instruction), and TED Talks are now standard fare at many colleges and universities. And students' interest in technology-based learning continues to grow. Throughout the 2000s, the percentage of U.S. students taking at least one online course rose steadily, growing from about 10% of college students in 2002 to 32% in 2010 (Allen & Seaman, 2011). This number is sure to increase as technological advances make online instruction even more accessible, multimodal, and user-friendly.

Today's students are also embracing service-learning and other similar pedagogies that allow them to actively connect their academic learning with issues in their communities. My university administers an annual survey to all of our undergraduate students and has consistently found that a large majority (over 80%) of University of Minnesota undergraduates believe that community engagement experiences that are connected to their academic learning are important. Similar strong support for community-based learning experiences among today's college students is found across the higher education spectrum, both in the United States and abroad (Global University Network for Innovation, 2014). This generation of students wants active learning experiences that allow them to apply their academic knowledge and skills to making meaningful contributions to society while also enhancing their academic achievement, personal development, and overall educational success (McGlynn, 2008; Black, 2010). Through pedagogies such as service-learning, which are academically rich and community-focused, students are offered the kinds of experiences that encourage their deeper engagement in the educational enterprise (Kuh, Kinzie, Schuh, & Whitt, 2010).

Given the growing popularity of both e-learning and service-learning, something powerful is likely to happen when these two educational practices converge. Indeed, as is described in this volume, eService-Learning has the potential to provide students with high-impact, transformative learning experiences. It is through this volume that we learn how eService-Learning contains features of both e-learning and service-learning, yet its essence is distinct from either of these foundational instructional practices. Like the emergence of a new color when two distinct colors are blended, eService-Learning takes the high-impact components of two different pedagogies to create a new, different, and unique educational experience for students.

As best practices for this potentially powerful pedagogy have begun to take shape, and the practice has found resonance across higher education institutions, a broad range of questions about the value and effectiveness of this instructional approach has also arisen. What exactly is eService-Learning? What makes it unique and different from other instructional practices? To what extent does eService-Learning live up to purported promise of improving students' educational experiences and outcomes? What extra efforts, on the part of the student, the faculty, the community, and/or the institution, are needed to ensure the implementation of a high-quality eService-Learning experience? Can eService-Learning fulfill the goals of both service-learning and e-learning, or must there be some compromise in the goals that can be achieved for each? What are the barriers and potential drawbacks to eService-Learning? How do colleges and universities embed and institutionalize eService-Learning within the curriculum?

These are just a few of the questions that *eService-Learning: Creating Experiential Learning and Civic Engagement Through Online and Hybrid Courses* addresses. Using educational practitioners' accounts of their own experiences in developing and implementing eService-Learning courses, this volume gives us an insiders' view into what eService-Learning is and is not, and what practitioners negotiate and consider as they incorporate eService-Learning into their curricula. It also reveals the potential of this innovative pedagogy for creating transformative and impactful educational experiences for students. While the volume speaks to the power and potential of eService-Learning to enhance classroom instruction, it also takes an honest and realistic look at eService-Learning's challenges and complexities. From examining different course formats for eService-Learning, to exploring ways of connecting new and emerging technologies to service-learning, to securing high-quality assessments in eService-Learning classrooms, this volume sheds light on a broad range of issues regarding both the strengths and limitations of this hybrid pedagogy.

Today's higher education faculty continue to face the realities of a rapidly changing educational and social environment. As they seek to integrate effective educational practices into their curricula, eService-Learning may emerge as a shining light that can guide them in meeting the many and complex goals of higher education. Whether or not eService-Learning ultimately lives up to its promise as a transformative pedagogy remains to be seen.

As one of the first volumes to explore the practice of eService-Learning, *eService-Learning: Creating Experiential Learning and Civic Engagement Through Online and Hybrid Courses* not only offers practitioners an understanding of this emerging pedagogy's essential elements, but it also explores important and key questions on the subject, laying the groundwork for further exploration and study. The field of eService-Learning is sure to gain prominence and popularity in the coming years. We will certainly look back at this book as a seminal volume that sought to unveil the power, complexity, and potential of this promising educational practice.

Andrew Furco
University of Minnesota

References

Allen, I.E. & Seaman, J. (2011). *Going the distance: Online education in the United States, 2011*. Babson Survey Research Group and Quahog Research Group, LLC. Babson Park, MA: Babson College.

Black, A. (2010). Gen Y: Who they are and how they learn. *Educational Horizons, 88*(2), 92–101.

Global University Network for Innovation (2014). *Higher education in the world 5: Knowledge, engagement and higher education: Contributing to social change*. GUNI Series on the Social Commitment of Universities. Barcelona: Technical University of Catalonia.

Kuh, G. D., Kinzie, J., Schuh, J. H., & Whitt, E. J. (2010). *Student success in college: Creating conditions that matter*. San Francisco: Jossey-Bass.

McGlynn, A. (2008). Millennials in college: How do we motivate them? *Education Digest, 73*(6), 19–22.

ACKNOWLEDGMENTS

From Katherine

I would like to thank my family for giving of themselves so that I could fulfill my passion and dreams. To my wonderful husband Gary: You are my best friend and the love of my life, always there to support me with unwavering patience, love, encouragement, friendship, and devotion. A special thanks to Marie Callender, who has become my husband's best dinner partner. To my beautiful daughter Kami and her husband JJ: Thank you for your love and support and for your continued work serving our country. To my talented son David and his wife Kristina: Thank you for always being there, your support and love, and your dedication to serving God and ministering to others. To my awesome and amazing grandchildren Samantha, Austin, Andrew, Ashton, Kyleigh, Garrison, and Jackson: You bring such love and joy to my life. And thanks to my parents Jean and Chuck Andrews, my grandfather Charles Irvin, and my brother Mike and his family, all of whom have played a role in laying the foundation for who I am today. Without my faith in God and my family's continued love, guidance, patience, support, encouragement, compassion, dedication, and inspiration, following my passion and fulfilling my dreams would not be possible. Always close at hand is the pocket dictionary my son gave me when I, as an adult learner at the age of 49, made the decision to return to school and complete my bachelor's degree. The inscription, which I hold dear to my heart, reads, "Dear Kid: I'm so proud of you for going to school. Keep it up! In Christ, David Nordyke." It was dated August 24, 2003. Since 2003, I not only accomplished obtaining my bachelor's degree but also obtained my master's degree, and I am now currently working on my doctoral degree. Thank you David for having that extra faith and confidence in me and for your inspiring words; going back to school changed my life forever.

To my dear colleagues and mentors Nathalie Rennell, Dr. Christie Brungardt, Don and Jane Cheek, Reverend Bob Hubbard, Elizabeth Strong, Mary Ann Wood, and Dr. Rachelle Darabi: Thank you for your unwavering support, encouragement, and leadership and your heartfelt wisdom, work ethic, and dedication to making the world a better place to live. Over the years you have served as my role models and educators, provided me with amazing opportunities, and continue to inspire me to follow my passion and dreams. To my lifelong friends Joanne Sherwood, Jane Carr, and Connie Vandre: Thank you for always being there for me; life is richer because of friends like you. To Missouri State University administrators, faculty, staff, and students: Thank you for your support and confidence in me and for providing me with the opportunity to serve the university.

To a very special lady, Dr. Harriet Cremeen: Reading your dissertation for your doctorate in education was encouraging, and I was taken with your wisdom about and your vision for experiential learning for students, especially the adult learner. I cannot tell you how appreciative I am of your friendship and your words of encouragement as I continue to pursue my doctorate in education.

And last, but certainly not least, to my coeditor, Dr. Jean Strait: Thank you! For without your faith and confidence in me, your mentorship and friendship, and your collaboration, dedication, and commitment to this book and the field of service-learning, this opportunity for me would not have been possible—my heartfelt thanks and appreciation. You, Jean Strait, are truly inspirational.

I am truly blessed and thank God daily for the wonderful life and opportunities He has given me. I am honored that I have the opportunity to share this book with those in the field of education and service-learning.

From Jean

It's book two, Joyce Jones! (Jonesy.) This book would not have happened without you. Thanks for your support, your love, and your patience. I love you like crazy! And Diana Jones, yes, editing is hard work; aren't you glad you have to edit only a few pages in sixth grade? I would like to thank my Pennsylvania family for guiding me into writing, especially my mother, Maureen Hoffman, who saved poems, songs, and stories I wrote when I was eight years old. Really, Mom, was it necessary to share them with my adult friends? I want to thank my Minnesota family for all the support and guidance they give every single day.

The past few years have been an incredible journey for me, and I would like to thank so many good friends and extended family. Gwen Pitsenbarger: You are my adopted mom! Thank you, and I love you. Julie and Amanda Pitsenbarger (Gracie and Sorin too): Thanks for holding me up when I fall and pushing me to keep standing up again. Patty Murphy: 20 years and counting! Rose and T: I love you! The Braun family, especially Jennifer and Marty, my crazy twins: Are you sick of hearing about the book? Well, it is finally done!

To all my friends at Pilgrim House Unitarian Universalist and North St. Paul Maplewood Oakdale Rotary Club: Social justice is love in action.

Most important, I would like to thank Kathy Nordyke. I told you that you could edit a book, and here it is! Seriously, I am so grateful for your friendship, your wit, and your everlasting optimism. Congratulations on your first book. You will just keep rising!

From Both

To the inspirational and dedicated leaders who have gone before us: Gandhi, Mother Teresa, John F. Kennedy, Martin Luther King Jr., and Nelson Mandela. Their work laid the foundation for leadership and service-learning, and it truly inspires us to appreciate what it means to make a difference in the world today—one step at a time. Thank you for being visionaries, leaders, and role models and for your unwavering quest to foster an appreciation for diversity, cultural competence, inclusion, and equality for all. We admire you for your values and beliefs and for taking a stand. It is evident in your work that one person can change the world and truly make a difference.

INTRODUCTION

Welcome to *eService-Learning: Creating Experiential Learning and Civic Engagement Through Online and Hybrid Courses.* It is our hope that this book will inspire you and provide you with a wealth of ideas, models, tools, and resources to assist you in creating civic engagement course work coupled with ideas for experiential learning opportunities, thus engaging your students in service-learning through the eService-Learning environment.

One of the latest trends in the field of higher education service-learning is eService-Learning. As referenced in chapter 3 of this book, eService-Learning removes boundaries associated with the more traditional method of service-learning. Unfortunately, as online teaching and learning has grown and evolved, there has been a lack of parallel innovative development in the field of civically engaged teaching and learning. As Waldner, McGorry, and Widener (2012) suggested, if higher education institutions are to remain relevant, service-learning must go online.

Keeping current and embracing 21st-century learning are essential to moving the needle forward in the field of civic engagement and service-learning. With this in mind, how do we move the needle forward? We do this by creating civic engagement and service-learning opportunities for students and embracing this online learning environment. Our goal is that the contents of this book will provide you with the essentials you need to embrace eService-Learning.

This book is divided into three primary sections, with two to five chapters in each section. Part one, "Essentials, Components, and Nuts and Bolts of eService-Learning," will provide you with the foundation for development and implementation of eService-Learning. Part two, "Models for eService-Learning," will provide you with a lens in which to view five different models from five universities across the United States that have developed and implemented effective eService-Learning courses. In part three, "Next Steps and Future Directions," you will gain insight into considerations for eService-Learning within higher education, as well as cautions about the process and action steps that should be taken when developing and implementing eService-Learning courses.

We are assuming that many of you will have an understanding of, and are familiar with, the definition of *civic engagement,* the pedagogy of service-learning, and how each element serves to enhance the other. For those of you new to the field of civic engagement and service-learning and who may be unfamiliar with the terms and pedagogy of both, chapter 1 provides you with an overview and explanation of how civic engagement and service-learning foster the student success, retention, skill, sensitivity, and commitment necessary for effective citizenship in a global world, engaging students in community-based problem solving and addressing social justice issues locally, nationally, and globally. In chapter 2, Leora Waldner discusses an understanding of how eService-Learning is an effective 21st-century learning tool and explores the models associated with eService-Learning. Chapter 3, by Katherine J. Nordyke, not only sets the stage for eService-Learning but also provides you with a road map for designing eService-Learning courses in the higher education setting and includes guides for developing outcomes and assessing the effectiveness of eService-Learning courses. In chapter 4, Jean Strait provides you with innovative ways to support eService-Learning through the use of technology, including moving from traditional reflection journals to ePortfolios to enhance the student's reflective experience.

As we move from the nuts and bolts of eService-Learning, chapters 5 through 9 take you on a journey, showcasing five universities' development and implementation of successful eService-Learning programs and courses utilizing the Hybrid I (Katherine J. Nordyke), Hybrid II (Pauline Mosley), and Hybrid III (Jean Strait) models; the Hybrid IV, Extreme eService-Learning model (Sue McGorry); and the mixed-model method (Paul H. Matthews). Learning from these universities and how they developed and implemented their eService-Learning course work and models will provide you with innovative and creative ideas that you can use within your university setting, programs, and service-learning courses.

Finally, chapters 10 (John Hamerlinck) and 11 (Jean Strait) focus on considerations for engaging in eService-Learning and provide you with cautions about developing and implementing eService-Learning, as well as action steps that should be taken when moving from traditional service-learning to eService-Learning.

It would be difficult to dispute the positive impact that service-learning has on students, not to mention the benefits of service-learning on student success and retention. The challenge is, however, in developing and implementing successful experiential eService-Learning opportunities for our students that truly move service-learning into 21st-century learning. We encourage you to explore the contents of this book in depth and then step out and explore the endless possibilities for developing and implementing your own eService-Learning course.

We hope that you enjoy the book, find value in our writings, and are inspired, motivated, and empowered to engage your students in the world of eService-Learning.

Reference

Waldner, L. S., McGorry, S. Y., & Widener, M. C. (2012). E-service-learning: The evolution of service-learning to engage a growing online student population. *Journal of Higher Education Outreach and Engagement, 16*(2), 123–150.

PART ONE

ESSENTIALS, COMPONENTS, AND NUTS AND BOLTS OF eSERVICE-LEARNING

I

PEDAGOGY OF CIVIC ENGAGEMENT, HIGH-IMPACT PRACTICES, AND eSERVICE-LEARNING

Jean Strait, Jane Turk, and Katherine J. Nordyke

Civic Engagement, Service-Learning, and Social Justice

For those new to the fields of civic engagement and service-learning and who may be unfamiliar with the terms and pedagogy of both, it is crucial to examine how civic engagement and service-learning (considered a high-impact educational practice) foster the student success, retention, skill, sensitivity, and commitment necessary for effective citizenship in a global world, engaging students in community-based problem solving and addressing social justice issues locally, nationally, and globally.

What Is Civic Engagement?

According to Ehrlich (2000), *civic engagement* means working to make a difference in the civic life of our communities and developing the combination of knowledge, skill, value, and motivation to make that difference. It means promoting the quality of life in a community through both political and nonpolitical processes. Saltmarsh (2005) explained that civic engagement occurs through the development of the capacity for engagement within students and citizens. This development can be taught and measured as *civic learning*.

If we think of civic learning as having the components of knowledge, skills, and values, we can get a better understanding of what it looks like.

So what knowledge, skills, and values do students gain through civic learning? *Civic knowledge* consists of political, historical, and civic knowledge gained from both academic and community engagement. A key ingredient for civic knowledge is historical knowledge that contextualizes community-based experiences (Saltmarsh, 2005). Students gain civic knowledge through their interaction with communities.

Civic skills are the general abilities students develop through community engagement, which include critical thinking, communication, public problem solving, civic judgment, civic imagination, creativity, and collaboration. *Civic values* include justice, participation, and inclusion (see Figure 1.1).

In the report *A Crucible Moment: College Learning and Democracy's Future*, the National Task Force on Civic Learning and Democratic Engagement (2012) outlined the ways in which civic knowledge, skills, and values and their collective action composed a framework for supporting and encouraging civic learning and democratic engagement in higher education. The framework expands the scope of civic learning beyond a familiar "civics" curriculum template that focused on passive reception of facts (e.g., identifying the three branches of government, one's legislators, and a short list of important events in U.S. history). Rather, the new framework of skills, knowledge, values, and collective action provides a broader definition and a more nuanced approach that stresses active engagement, application, and participation. According to *A Crucible Moment* (McTighe Musil, 2012), to revitalize civic engagement through a 21st-century framework of college

Figure 1.1 Civic Learning Incorporates Civic Skills, Knowledge, and Values

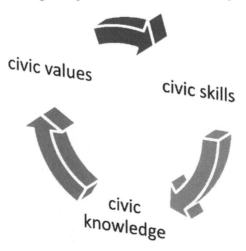

Figure 1.2 Framework for 21st-Century Civic Learning

Knowledge

- Familiarity with key demographic texts and universal democratic principles, and with selected debates—in U.S. and other societies—concerning their applications
- Historic and sociological understanding of several democratic movements, both U.S.and abroad
- Understanding one's sources of identity and their influence on civic values, assumptions, and responsibilities to a wider public
- Knowledge of the diverse cultures, histories, values, and contestations that have shaped U.S. and other world societies
- Exposure to multiple religious traditions and to alterative views about the relation between religion and government
- Knowledge of the political systems that frame constitutional democracies and of political levers for influencing change

Skills

- Critical inquiry, analysis, and reasoning
- Quantitative reasoning
- Gathering and evaluating multiple sources of evidence
- Seeking, engaging, and being informed by multiple perspectives
- Deliberation and bridge building across differences
- Collaborative decision making
- Ability to communicate in multiple languages

Values

- Respect for freedom and human dignity
- Empathy
- Open-mindedness
- Tolerance
- Justice
- Equality
- Ethical integrity
- Responsibility to a larger good

Collective Action

- Integration of knowledge, skills, and examined values to inform actions taken in concert with other people
- Moral discernment and behavior
- Navigation of political systems and processes, both formal and informal
- Public problem solving with diverse partners
- Compromise, civility, and mutual respect

Note. From *A Crucible Moment: College Learning and Democracy's Future* by Caryn McTighe Musil. Copyright 2012 by the Association of American Colleges and Universities." Reprinted with permission.

learning (see Figure 1.2), students "need to understand how their political system works and how to influence it, certainly, but they also need to understand the cultural and global contexts in which democracy is both deeply valued and deeply contested" and is applicable from K–12 all the way through college and university academic programs.

How Is Civic Engagement Taught?

The underlying aim of civic engagement is to produce meaningful service and experience for all involved participants. The relationship among all involved parties is ideally reciprocal: The community partners explain their needs; the students and faculty work with the community partners to find a sustainable way to address their needs; and the experience serves as a common ground for students to enhance their scholarship, raise questions, and explore alternative solutions with new social consciousness, not only in the classroom but also as they move into the world as professionals.

Civic engagement can be facilitated through several pedagogies. The Wheel of Civic Engagement, shown in Figure 1.3, highlights seven different civic engagement pedagogies, service-learning being among them. Pedagogy can be thought of as a teaching method or strategy of teaching. For example, if we want to teach civic engagement through service-learning, our end goals

Figure 1.3 Wheel of Civic Engagement

Note. Adapted from Cotterman (2003).

include civic knowledge, skills, and values. We get to those goals by teaching service-learning. Depending on what the end goal is for civic engagement, a teacher may need to use one or more pedagogies to reach the outcome. Table 1.1 lists a few pedagogies from the Wheel of Civic Engagement and highlights the purpose and examples of each.

What Is Service-Learning?

According to the National Youth Leadership Council (2014b), service-learning is a multifaceted teaching and learning process. Though each service-learning project is uniquely tailored to meet specific learning goals and community needs, several common elements are critical for success.

A brief review of the research done on service-learning over the past 20 years highlights basic commonalities within the practice. Essentially, learning becomes experiential. Students apply their skills through the school curriculum. Service-learning practice traditionally has four types of implementation. These include direct service-learning, indirect service-learning, research-based service-learning, and advocacy-based service-learning as identified originally by the National Service-Learning Clearinghouse (2013) as

TABLE 1.1
Pedagogies of Community Engagement

Pedagogy	*Definitions*
Community-based research	Researching and gathering information on areas of need as defined by a community
Service-learning	Connecting real-world experiences with academic goals; service benefits the community partner, and the learning benefits the student
Community partnerships	Well-planned, thoughtful discussions with topics and agendas; can be workshops, community meetings, even online open discussions
Internships	Practical application of theory learned in an academic setting but provided in a controlled setting for students to "try on" the profession
Activism	Increasing community awareness through advocacy through both public and media avenues
Volunteerism and community service	Usually a onetime experience working on an important issue or need

referenced by the University of Central Arkansas (http://uca.edu/service-learning/types/) and the National Youth Leadership Council (NYLC; 2005).

The following in an extract from the University of Central Arkansas (2013) website, which is based on information the university obtained from the National Service-Learning Clearinghouse.

Direct service-learning is person-to-person, face-to-face service projects in which the students' service directly impacts individuals who receive the service from the students. Examples include the following:

- Tutoring other students and adults
- Conducting art, music, or dance lessons for younger students
- Helping other students resolve conflict
- Giving performances on violence and drug prevention
- Creating lessons and presenting them to younger students
- Creating life reviews for hospice patients

The impact on skills practiced by servers include the following: caring for others, personal responsibility, dependability, interpersonal skills, ability to get along with others who are different, problem-solving, beginning-to-end, big-picture learning.

Indirect service-learning practice focuses on broad issues, environmental projects, and community development projects that have clear benefits to the community or environment but not necessarily to individual identified people with whom the students are working. Examples include the following:

- Compiling a town history
- Restoring historic structures or building low-income housing
- Removing exotic plants and restoring ecosystems, preparing preserve areas for public use

The impact on skills practiced by servers include the following: cooperating, learning teamwork skills, playing different roles, organizing, prioritizing, and obtaining project-specific skills.

Research-based service-learning gathers and presents information on areas of interest and need. These projects find, gather, and report on information that is needed. Examples include the following:

- Writing a guide on available community services and translating it into Spanish and other languages of new residents
- Conducting longitudinal studies of local bodies of water; doing water testing for local residents
- Gathering information and creating brochures or videos for nonprofit or government agencies
- Mapping state lands and monitoring flora and fauna
- Conducting surveys, studies, evaluations, experiments, interviews, and so on

The impact on skills practiced by servers include the following: learning how to learn, getting answers, finding information, making discriminating judgments, working systematically, obtaining organizational skills, and learning how to assess, evaluate, and test hypotheses.

Finally, *advocacy service-learning* practice educates others about topics of public interest. These projects aim to create awareness and action on some issue that is in the public interest. Examples include the following:

- Planning and putting on public forums on topics of interest in the community
- Conducting public information campaigns on topics of interest or local needs
- Working with elected officials to draft legislation to improve communities
- Training the community in fire safety or disaster preparation

The impact on skills practiced by servers include the following: learning perseverance; understanding rules, systems, and processes; practicing engaged citizenship; and working with adults. (*Note.* As cited in University of Central Arkansas, 2015 http://uca.edu/servicelearning/types/. The National Service-Learning Clearinghouse website is no longer available; however, the information is on the University of Central Arkansas website, http://uca.edu/servicelearning/types.)

Seven Elements of High-Quality Service-Learning

Preiser-Houy and Navarrete (2006) proposed an integrated, multidimensional concept of student learning that linked the academic with personal and interpersonal learning outcomes. They labeled the following seven elements: integrated learning, high-quality service, collaboration, student voice, civic responsibility, reflection, and evaluation. These elements are explained next.

Integrated Learning

The service-learning project has clearly articulated knowledge, skill, or value goals that arise from broader classroom and institution goals. The service informs the academic learning content, and the academic learning content informs the service. Life skills learned outside the classroom are integrated back into learning.

High-Quality Service

The service responds to an actual community need that is recognized by the community. The service is age appropriate and well organized. The service is designed to achieve significant benefits for students and the community.

Collaboration

The service-learning project is a collaboration among as many of these partners as is feasible: students, community-based organization staff, support staff, administrators, faculty, and recipients of service. All partners benefit from the project and contribute to its planning.

Student Voice

Students participate actively in choosing and planning the service project; planning and implementing the reflection sessions, evaluation, and celebration; and taking on roles and tasks that are appropriate for their age.

Civic Responsibility

The service-learning project promotes students' responsibility to care for others and contribute to the community. By participating in the service-learning project, students understand how they can impact their community.

Reflection

Reflection establishes connections between students' service experiences and the academic curriculum. Reflection occurs before, during, and after the service-learning project.

Evaluation

All the partners, especially students, are involved in evaluating the service-learning project. The evaluation seeks to measure progress toward the learning and service goals of the project.

What Are High-Impact Educational Practices?

George Kuh (2008) developed the framework of high-impact educational practices in collaboration with the Association of American Colleges and Universities (AAC&U) as part of the AAC&U's Liberal Education and America's Promise (LEAP) initiative. Building on the AAC&U's previously identified set of effective educational practices and essential liberal education learning outcomes, Kuh analyzed data gathered from the National Survey of Student Engagement to determine which of the effective educational practices fostered deep student learning and enhanced student retention rates, particularly in underserved student populations.

The resulting set of 10 high-impact educational practices included first-year seminars and experiences, common intellectual experiences, learning communities, writing-intensive courses, collaborative assignments and projects, undergraduate research, diversity/global learning, community-based learning and service-learning, internships, and capstone experiences.

In the 2008 AAC&U report *High-Impact Educational Practices: What They Are, Who Has Access to Them, and Why They Matter* (see Figure 1.4), Kuh identified the following reasons why schools interested in increasing student engagement, learning, and retention should place a premium on high-impact educational practices: First, the practices incorporate *purposeful tasks* for students to concentrate on; second, the practices encourage *meaningful and frequent interaction* between students and the faculty instructor; third, a subset of these practices places students in the position *to build relationships with people different from themselves*, an especially salient trait in field- or community-based work inherent in service-learning, internship, and study abroad experiences; fourth, the practices incorporate *frequent feedback* for students; fifth, several of the practices enable students to take their learning out of the confines of the traditional classroom and *see application of knowledge and skills in a variety of contexts*; and sixth, high-impact educational practices can often be life changing, allowing students to understand themselves and their relationship to the world around them in fresh and inspiring ways.

Kuh found that high-impact educational practices played a particularly important role in fostering student success—including increased of retention and graduation rates and even higher grade point averages—in historically underserved populations. However, Kuh also found that access to high-impact educational practices was often limited to students already well served by the conventional undergraduate experience. As such, Kuh recommended that every college or university make high-impact educational practices available across the student population with the explicit goal of every student having access to at least one high-impact educational practice per year of enrollment.

Why Is Service-Learning Considered a High-Impact Educational Practice?

In 2010, the AAC&U issued a follow-up report on a subset of high-impact educational practices titled *Five High-Impact Practices: Research on Learning Outcomes, Completion, and Quality* (Brownell & Swaner, 2010). Service-learning was one of the five practices highlighted in the report, which found that service-learning led to several gains for participating students, including enhanced academic engagement (especially regarding the application of course knowledge and skills), improved critical thinking and writing skills, increased interaction with faculty, and increased sense of civic engagement and reduction in stereotyping.

The gains found in the 2010 AAC&U report are logical when put into the context of effective service-learning project and course design. When implemented according to best practices, a service-learning approach can incorporate all six characteristics of effective high-impact educational practices. The academic integration of knowledge centers around completing a *purposeful task*—whether it is direct service, a physical artifact, or another working arrangement—developed in consultation with the community partner.

Service-learning projects and courses also incorporate tremendous opportunities for *meaningful and frequent interaction* both with the larger community and in the classroom. Active collaboration with a community partner allows students to *build relationships with people different from themselves* and includes opportunities for students to actively see and shape ways in which *academic knowledge and skills are applied in a variety of contexts*.

As is the case with experiential learning in general, the learning gains that a service-learning approach provides requires students' active, structured reflection and analysis of their experiences in the community context and their work in collaboration with the community partner and their peers. *Frequent feedback* between student peers and from the faculty instructor also moves reflection and learning to increasingly deeper levels over the duration of the project or course (see Figure 1.4).

Finally, at the culmination of a successful service-learning project or course, the world of the students' own experiences and identities can converge in meaningful ways with their work on campus and within a larger

Figure 1.4 AAC&U High-Impact Educational Practices

High-Impact Educational Practices
★ ★ ★ ★ ★ ★ ★ ★ ★ ★ ★

First-Year Seminars and Experiences

Many schools now build into the curriculum first-year seminars or other programs that bring small groups of students together with faculty or staff on a regular basis. The highest-quality first-year experiences place a strong emphasis on critical inquiry, frequent writing, information literacy, collaborative learning, and other skills that develop students' intellectual and practical competencies. First-year seminars can also involve students with cutting-edge questions in scholarship and with faculty members' own research.

Common Intellectual Experiences

The older idea of a "core" curriculum has evolved into a variety of modern forms, such as a set of required common courses or a vertically organized general education program that includes advanced integrative studies and/or required participation in a learning community (see below). These programs often combine broad themes—e.g., technology and society, global interdependence—with a variety of curricular and cocurricular options for students.

Learning Communities

The key goals for learning communities are to encourage integration of learning across courses and to involve students with "big questions" that matter beyond the classroom. Students take two or more linked courses as a group and work closely with one another and with their professors. Many learning communities explore a common topic and/or common readings through the lenses of different disciplines. Some deliberately link "liberal arts" and "professional courses"; others feature service learning.

Writing-Intensive Courses

These courses emphasize writing at all levels of instruction and across the curriculum, including final-year projects. Students are encouraged to produce and revise various forms of writing for different audiences in different disciplines. The effectiveness of this repeated practice "across the curriculum" has led to parallel efforts in such areas as quantitative reasoning, oral communication, information literacy, and, on some campuses, ethical inquiry.

Collaborative Assignments and Projects

Collaborative learning combines two key goals: learning to work and solve problems in the company of others, and sharpening one's own understanding by listening seriously to the insights of others, especially those with different backgrounds and life experiences. Approaches range from study groups within a course, to team-based assignments and writing, to cooperative projects and research.

Undergraduate Research

Many colleges and universities are now providing research experiences for students in all disciplines. Undergraduate research, however, has been most prominently used in science disciplines. With strong support from the National Science Foundation and the research community, scientists are reshaping their courses to connect key concepts and questions with students' early and active involvement in systematic investigation and research. The goal is to involve students with actively contested questions, empirical observation, cutting-edge technologies, and the sense of excitement that comes from working to answer important questions.

Diversity/Global Learning

Many colleges and universities now emphasize courses and programs that help students explore cultures, life experiences, and worldviews different from their own. These studies—which may address U.S. diversity, world cultures, or both—often explore "difficult differences" such as racial, ethnic, and gender inequality, or continuing struggles around the globe for human rights, freedom, and power. Frequently, intercultural studies are augmented by experiential learning in the community and/or by study abroad.

Service Learning, Community-Based Learning

In these programs, field-based "experiential learning" with community partners is an instructional strategy—and often a required part of the course. The idea is to give students direct experience with issues they are studying in the curriculum and with ongoing efforts to analyze and solve problems in the community. A key element in these programs is the opportunity students have to both apply what they are learning in real-world settings and reflect in a classroom setting on their service experiences. These programs model the idea that giving something back to the community is an important college outcome, and that working with community partners is good preparation for citizenship, work, and life.

Internships

Internships are another increasingly common form of experiential learning. The idea is to provide students with direct experience in a work setting—usually related to their career interests—and to give them the benefit of supervision and coaching from professionals in the field. If the internship is taken for course credit, students complete a project or paper that is approved by a faculty member.

Capstone Courses and Projects

Whether they're called "senior capstones" or some other name, these culminating experiences require students nearing the end of their college years to create a project of some sort that integrates and applies what they've learned. The project might be a research paper, a performance, a portfolio of "best work," or an exhibit of artwork. Capstones are offered both in departmental programs and, increasingly, in general education as well.

LEAP

Note: From *High-Impact Educational Practices: What They Are, Who Has Access to Them, and Why They Matter* by George D. Kuh. Copyright 2008 by the Association of American Colleges and Universities. Reprinted with permission.

community context. This will enable fresh insight and an empowering confidence about the difference that they can make in collaboration with others and the community around them.

The authors of the 2010 AAC&U report noted that further research is needed on the ways in which service-learning can be made more accessible to underserved student populations and that the self-selection bias and short duration of many service-learning projects can make service-learning less effective. That said, with careful design, implementation, and an increase in student access, service-learning holds the potential to be among the most effective high-impact pedagogical strategies to increase student success across the board.

What If I Am an Online Teacher Who Is New to Service-Learning? Where Do I Start?

Many skilled online teachers have asked me where and how they start with service-learning. I usually answer this question by focusing on preparation and logistics for each service-learning project and considering the two major groups that will need them, the students and the community partners. Service-learning requires a set of skills from participants that they may or may not possess. Developing skill sets for teamwork and cultural competence is essential. A structured reflection process assists all participants, but this is something that should be created well before any service-learning takes place. Students need to learn how to evaluate not only what they are learning but also how they are impacting the community and helping them meet their goals.

For those starting a new service-learning project with a class, I suggest using a checklist of what to consider when planning and what kinds of skills need to be developed (see Table 1.2). For example, if I have students working with fifth graders in reading, I need to determine how they will work in teams and what skills they will need to develop to model effective teamwork for the fifth graders. I often run simulations where students practice with each other what they will do in the field. This helps me see what they can do and what they need help developing. I have participants brainstorm using my checklist as a reflective tool after the simulation. The more everyone can be a part of the initial process, the greater investment they will have in the project and each other.

Making the Case for eService-Learning

The beauty of eService-Learning is that it already possesses the potential to offer all the high-impact practices that regular service-learning does. One of its strengths is making service-learning accessible to underserved populations through electronic means. Cost areas in regular service-learning become nonissues. Items such as transportation costs and meeting space requirements can virtually be eliminated. Both service and learning can be tailored specifically to optimize learning and service for all involved. Even though many of the authors in this text have been working with variations of

TABLE 1.2
Preplanning Guide for Service-Learning Skill Development

Skills	Students	Community
Teamwork		
Cultural competency		
Structuring the reflection process		
Evaluating the service-learning	(student learning outcomes)	(goals of the community)

eService-Learning for at least a decade, it is just now being investigated as a potential mainstream pedagogy. With eService-Learning, the possibilities are limitless, and as more research is completed in this area, we are certain that it will be regarded as a 21st-century high-impact educational practice.

References

Brownell, J. E., & Swaner, L. E. (2010). *Five high-impact practices: Research on learning outcomes, completion, and quality*. Washington, DC: Association of American Colleges and Universities.

Cotterman, K. (2003). *The Wheel of Civic Engagement.* Retrieved February 23, 2013, from National Louis University: http://nlu.nl.edu/cec/whatis.cfm

Ehrlich, T. (2000). *Civic responsibility and higher education.* Santa Barbara, CA: Greenwood.

Kuh, G. D. (2008). *High-impact educational practices: What they are, who has access to them, and why they matter.* Washington, DC: Association of American Colleges and Universities.

McTighe Musil, C., & National Task Force on Civic Learning and Democratic Engagement. (2012). *A crucible moment: College learning and democracy's future.* Washington, DC: Association of American Colleges and Universities. Retrieved March 5, 2014, from https://www.aacu.org/crucible

National Youth Leadership Council. (2014a). *Service-Learning tip sheet: Types of service.* Retrieved March 5, 2014, from http://www.nylc.org/sites/nylc.org/files/files/48TipType.pdf

National Youth Leadership Council. (2014b). *What is service-learning?* Retrieved March 5, 2014, from www.nylc.org

Preiser-Houy, L., & Navarrete, C. J. (2006). Exploring the learning in service-learning: A case of a community-based research project in web-based systems development. *Journal of Information Systems Education, 17*(3), 273–284.

Saltmarsh, J. (2005). The civic promise of service learning. *Liberal Education, 91*(2), 50–55.

University of Central Arkansas (UCA). (2013). *Service learning types.* As cited from National Service-Learning Clearinghouse at http:///www.servicelearning.org/. Retrieved March 5, 2014, from http://uca.edu/servicelearning/types/

2

---

eSERVICE-LEARNING

Breaking Through the Barrier

Leora Waldner

eService-Learning is not just a class—it is a calling. eService-Learning provides online students with opportunities for hands-on community service that deepens their engagement with course theories and, thus, learning outcomes. eService-Learning is not a "substitute" for traditional service-learning, done only as a medium of last resort when an instructor is forced online. Rather, eService-Learning is its own full-bodied medium and, in some cases, has the potential to *outperform* traditional service-learning on several dimensions because of its inherent digital grounding.

This chapter introduces the fundamentals of eService-Learning, exploring what it is, how it is done, and why it is done. We briefly explore the types of eService-Learning and its essential components. The chapter also demonstrates why eService-Learning is the perfect vehicle for delivering 21st-century skills—skills today's students will need to thrive in tomorrow's demanding professional environment.

eService-Learning remains a relatively rare phenomenon in online instruction. Thus, we explore two common barriers to eService-Learning: traditional service-learning instructors who are new to online learning and not sure how to translate their service-learning endeavors into a viable online experience, and online instructors who have never attempted service-learning yet wish to incorporate eService-Learning into their online instructional portfolio. By providing examples, we create a road map to overcome those barriers. Finally, we explore how *institutions* can systematically integrate and encourage eService-Learning as a vital core component of their online offerings.

eService-Learning in Action

Mr. Connor Stanton needs help. His newly established nonprofit organization, Thrive Appalachia, serves at-risk youth in the highly impoverished region in which he resides. Yet his board of directors lacks direction, unsure of which services to provide. Should they focus on educational mentoring programs? Community development? Recreational opportunities? Connor knows the nonprofit should conduct a needs assessment to determine funding and operational priorities, but he lacks the resources (both financial and expertise) to conduct that kind of assessment.

Dr. Shameka Johnston faces a challenge of an entirely different nature. She is a true instructional genius, and she teaches the best marketing strategy class at Miller-Keys University. Though the class is online, Dr. Johnston uses discussion boards, blogs, live webinars, and other interactive tools to foster engagement in her marketing strategy class. Despite her stellar course evaluations, Dr. Johnston is not satisfied. She wants a tool to foster complete *immersion* in the subject so the students can profoundly experience marketing strategy on a new level.

By combining service-learning and online learning, eService-Learning can solve both of their dilemmas. Connor's organization taps the resources of a prestigious university, arranging with the faculty to design and pilot test a needs assessment as part of a graduate-level program evaluation course, at no cost to the organization. Thrive Appalachia receives a ready-to-launch needs assessment as part of the service-learning partnership, and on the basis of that needs assessment, the organization chooses to focus on economic development as a key priority. In turn, the students gain hands-on experience from developing that needs assessment, a skill they can place on their résumés. That hands-on experience also intimately tied into the student learning outcomes for the course, allowing the students to more deeply understand the theories of program evaluation.

Dr. Johnston decides to challenge her online marketing strategy students to create a top-notch marketing plan for a rural nonprofit that wants to market local women's crafts online. The student learning outcomes and course evaluations were off-the-charts good. Dr. Johnston discovered that the students absorbed the theories of marketing on a whole new level and had a new skill to place on their résumé. Best yet, the nonprofit received a first-rate marketing strategy, developed by the students under Dr. Johnston's tutelage, to help it focus on its future target market.

Though fictional, these two examples demonstrate the power of eService-Learning to overcome geographical limitations while equipping online learning with a powerful technique to engage students. eService-Learning—"the marriage of service-learning with online learning" (Waldner, McGorry, & Widener, 2012)—allows the burgeoning ranks of online students to experience the benefits of service-learning, even in a fully online class.

eService-Learning: What Is It?

What is service-learning? The National Service-Learning Clearinghouse (2013) defined *service-learning* as "a teaching and learning strategy that integrates meaningful community service with instruction and reflection to enrich the learning experience, teach civic responsibility, and strengthen communities." Service-learning allows students of all ages to *apply* what they learn in the classroom to solve real-world problems, thus enhancing learning while actively contributing to the community.

eService-Learning combines service-learning and online learning. Specifically, eService-Learning is a service-learning course wherein the instruction and/or the service occur partially or fully online (Waldner et al., 2012). Examples of an eService-Learning class include an online grant-writing class drafting grants for a community partner, an in-class informational technology class building online communities for an autism group, an online education class in Minnesota providing virtual mentoring to at-risk students in New Orleans, and so on. Potential eService-Learning applications exist in numerous disciplines (Figure 2.1 provides examples). Importantly, these classes can effectively bridge the geography gap, allowing an engineering student in Alaska to serve a community in Africa, or an environmental policy student in Japan to research potential best practices for urban-wildlife corridors in Southern California. eService-Learning literally creates a world of opportunities to connect students with communities across the globe—or at their very own doorstep.

According to Eyler, Giles, Stenson, and Gray (2001), benefits of service-learning can include personal outcomes such as moral development or enhanced personal efficacy and leadership skills (Wang, 2000). Service-learning can also increase racial understanding and instill a commitment to service and sense of social responsibility (Harkavy & Hartley, 2010). Service-learning can also positively impact academic learning outcomes and critical analysis skills by enabling students to apply knowledge in practical settings (Eyler & Giles, 1999). Service-learning also promotes development of professional skills (Bennett, Henson, & Drane, 2003; Simons & Cleary, 2006). Service-learning can benefit not only the college by ensuring civic engagement and partnering with

Figure 2.1 Potential eService-Learning Applications

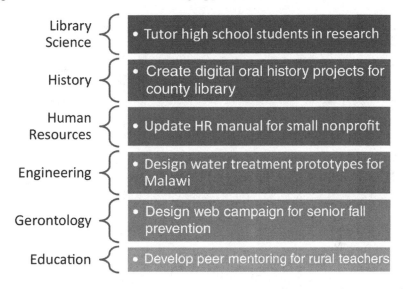

Library Science { • Tutor high school students in research

History { • Create digital oral history projects for county library

Human Resources { • Update HR manual for small nonprofit

Engineering { • Design water treatment prototypes for Malawi

Gerontology { • Design web campaign for senior fall prevention

Education { • Develop peer mentoring for rural teachers

the community but also the instructor by providing community or departmental service opportunities and potentially enhanced course evaluations.

In addition to those benefits, eService-Learning can allow students anywhere, regardless of geography, physical constraints, work schedule, or other access limitations, to experience service-learning. It also equips online learning with a powerful tool to engage students; engagement poses one of the most significant challenges in online learning (Gaytan & McEwen, 2007; Hill, Song, & West, 2009; Muirhead, 2004; Swan, 2002). However, eService-Learning does have limitations, most notably, technology challenges; difficulties sustaining three-way communication among the instructor, community partner, and students; and added workload for the instructor (Killian, 2004; Malvey, Hamby, & Fottler, 2006; Waldner et al., 2012).

As with traditional service-learning, in eService-Learning the service *must* connect to the learning. Service-learning also should include reflection to allow students to more fully integrate the experiential knowledge and tie it into course theories. In eService-Learning, the core components of service, learning, and reflection may take a different form because of the online medium; for example, reflection often occurs through discussion board interactions, journals, wikis, or blogs in an eService-Learning course. Moreover, the service, though still community based, may reflect a broader global or professional community rather than the local physical community. Nonetheless, the core elements remain (see Figure 2.2).

Figure 2.2 Core Components

Service	• Significant community-based work defined in response to a need or aspiration presented by one or more partnering community organizations and for which core issues of impact, sustainability, and reciprocity have been addressed.
Clear Linkage	• Clear linkage between the service and course learning goals, including both academic and civic learning, which is communicated to students in the syllabus.
Preparation	• A plan to prepare students for the roles they will occupy, including preparation to respectfully engage with a community that may not be their own and to work with people who may differ from them significantly in terms of race, class, or other elements of social identity.
Structured Reflection	• A plan to engage students in systematic reflection on their experience in the community—through talking, writing, or other means—in order to make of their experience a text for the course, taking from it key points of understanding, and to link it with their learning from other course materials.
Evaluation	• Evaluation of the service, learning, and partnership: at a minimum, a plan (a) for assessing whether the students' service provides something of value to the community, (b) for assessing what students learn from this combination of service and academic work, and (c) for evaluating the partnership between the course and the community organization(s).

Note. Adapted from University of Massachusetts at Amherst Civic Engagement and Service-Learning (2013).

Are There Different Types of eService-Learning?

Traditional service-learning (a class where the instruction and service are conducted entirely on-site) has been extensively studied. eService-Learning, as an emerging medium, is less well understood. Waldner et al. (2012) identified four emerging types of eService-Learning: the Extreme eService-Learning and three distinct forms of hybrids, wherein instruction and/or service are partially online.

In contrast to traditional service-learning, *Extreme eService-Learning* describes a fully online class where 100% of the instruction and 100% of the service occur online (see Figure 2.3). In chapter 8 of this book, Sue McGorry describes an MBA Extreme eService-Learning class wherein the instructor and students partnered with a new nonprofit dedicated to fostering lifelong learning in public safety. The students developed a promotional plan to build awareness of the new nonprofit, which was formed to honor a fallen public safety officer.

Malvey et al. (2006) also described an excellent example of a health care class where students updated human resources policies for a not-for-profit acute care facility. Students began by auditing the policies for regulatory compliance, then conducted interviews with senior and middle management staff using chat rooms, and concluded by presenting their revised policies on a discussion board. Malvey et al. also described an online finance course that successfully created a zero-based budget for a local county health department. Other examples of Extreme eService-Learning include an online marketing class that created marketing materials for an Alabama humane society (Hunter, 2007) and an online graduate policy analysis class that conducted best practices research on health disparities for a local county in Georgia (Waldner, Roberts, Widener, & Sullivan, 2011).

These Extreme eService-Learning courses often constitute client-based courses (Waldner & Hunter, 2008), focusing on creating a tangible and well-defined product (policy analysis, grant, etc.) for the community partner (client) within the specified course time frame. These courses often rely on real-time webinars or other virtual synchronous and asynchronous communication with the community partner to ensure students obtain

Figure 2.3 Continuum of Service-Learning

Note. See Waldner et al. (2010).

the information they need to develop a useful product and to present that product to the community partner. We might characterize these courses as *transactional* rather than *transformational* (Burns, 1978; Clayton, Bringle, Senor, Huq, & Morrison, 2010; Enos & Morton, 2003). Whereas transactional relationships focus on completing a short-term task, transformational relationships feature longer term, sustained interaction wherein the parties grow and change because of that deeper relationship. Though Extreme eService-Learning may foster some measure of appreciation for social justice, the primary intent is often to supply the community partner (nonprofit or government client) with a useful product—an *artifact*, if you will.

Beyond Extreme eService-Learning courses, the three other types of eService-Learning courses are hybrids (see Figure 2.4). In Hybrid I, the *instruction* is fully online; in Hybrid II, the *service* is fully online. Hybrid III represents a true blended hybrid eService-Learning course, with aspects of both the instruction and the service on-site and online.

The *Hybrid I model (instruction online)* features an online class wherein the service is conducted locally on-site, thus allowing students to experience hands-on service in a local context. Chapter 5 of this book, authored by Katherine J. Nordyke, describes the First-Year Experience course at Missouri State University that utilizes the Hybrid I model, combining online instruction with on-site service. Though the course work was online, the students completed a 15-hour service-learning placement in their respective communities to allow them to select civic issues of interest to them, such as homelessness, literacy, or disaster relief.

Figure 2.4 Four Emerging Types of eService-Learning

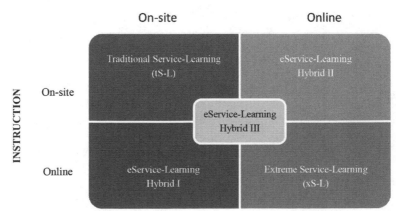

Note. Modified from Waldner et al. (2012).

In Bennett and Green's (2001) example, online sports management students conducted their service with a local organization, such as a local school or athletic association. Instruction (as well as reflection and evaluation) occurred online. Guthrie and McCracken (2010) examined a leadership course that explored community engagement and social change. The course, taught entirely online, required students to complete individual action plans with 60 hours of local community service. Because this involved the instructor coordinating with a number of different agencies and partners (with ensuing supervisory challenges), this version of the Hybrid I model remains relatively rare.

A second variation on Hybrid I involves international field travel, such as Burton's (2003) field experience course, conducted online with a 10-day intensive hands-on group experience in Guatemala. This course allowed the students to further implement the products they had developed during the online portion of the course (e.g., web page of village goods for sale, review of village health conditions).

Both variations of Hybrid I demonstrate the potential of eService-Learning to serve local and international nonprofits in a physical hands-on manner, regardless of where the students actually live. It does so by concentrating on the hands-on service-learning portion, either locally with multiple service partners or internationally with a partner community. This hybrid type is more *transformational* in nature, allowing for fully immersed service, rather than transactional. Generally speaking, this type of eService-Learning is designed to cultivate appreciation of either social justice matters or a professional workplace setting and is not geared exclusively to creating a product.

The *Hybrid II model (service online)* features an on-site class where the service is 100% online. This hybrid typically occurs in a computing resources, information technology, or web design course, and it tasks students with building online resources such as websites and the like.

As an example, Lazar and Preece (1999) described an information system course that challenged students to develop online communities for a Down syndrome advocacy group. Mosley and Pennachio (2005) highlighted a web design class that created highly usable websites for a local school district. Thus, the service is the website or online resource, and students learn by developing the product, assessing its usability, implementing and managing it, and reflecting on the experience.

Interestingly enough, in the Hybrid II model, the students and the service-learning partner often both reside in the same local community. However, as the eService-Learning medium emerges, this hybrid type may well emerge to feature on-site courses with students providing online products for faraway community partners. We can consider this hybrid type more *transactional* in nature than transformative, as it is designed to produce a discrete product or artifact rather than a transformational understanding about another community or issue.

The *Hybrid III model (blended)* refers to a blended class that offers instruction and service partially on-site and partially online. These blended Hybrid III types cover a large range of courses, thus they can be either transactional (such as the Killian course) or transformational depending on the specific design of the course and the degree of student immersion in the service setting. The Each One, Teach One program (Strait & Jones, 2009), discussed further by Jean Strait in chapter 7 of this text, combines on-site instruction with innovative online communication, allowing Hamline University students and students at the Avalon High School in St. Paul, Minnesota, to mentor students in grades five through nine at a New Orleans school. The Hamline and Avalon students paired to lead groups of students as a team. Initial contact occurred by phone and online. Subsequently, students traveled to New Orleans for a 10-day on-site service working session.

Other examples of a Hybrid III type include a course (Killian, 2004) where the initial instruction occurred on-site and the subsequent service component occurred online, with the students developing grant proposals, strategic plans, and best practices and reconvening on-site to present the products to the client. A nursing course (Blackwell, 2008) combined on-site clinical experience with online and on-site instruction so that students could have hands-on experience delivering holistic nursing care in a community-based setting, such as school clinics, psychiatric crisis units, and long-term care facilities. Bemidji State University's teacher training program, the Distributed Learning in Teacher Education (DLiTE), featured weekend face-to-face classroom experiences with professors twice during the semester, along with online instruction in pedagogy, language arts, and science methods, with some classes requiring students to arrange their own eService-Learning placements at summer school programs, local libraries, and other locales (Strait & Sauer, 2004).

eService-Learning and the three hybrid types may result in strikingly different service or course learning outcomes. For example, one might expect less civic engagement in Extreme eService-Learning, with its limited product delivery, thus we might expect it to be more transactional in nature. In the Hybrid I model, students conduct hands-on service on-site, thus they presumably are immersed more in the local agency or community settings. Hybrid I courses, particularly those such as the Service Oriented Field Experience described by Burton (2003), with travel to and service in Guatemala, may have more potential to be transformational in nature. Each type of eService-Learning may also face different technical limitations and require different techniques to optimize service-learning outcomes.

Why eService-Learning Might Outperform Traditional Service-Learning Courses

eService-Learning makes an ideal vehicle for teaching 21st-century skills. Proponents of 21st-century skill building suggest that today's students will need a radically different set of skills than what was needed by previous generations (Partnership for 21st Century Skills, 2009). "Within the context of core knowledge instruction, students must also learn the essential skills for success in today's world, such as critical thinking, problem solving, communication and collaboration" (Partnership for 21st Century Skills, 2013). Lectures and rote memorization will no longer suffice for this generation of learners. In short, students cannot just listen; they must *do*.

Specifically, to develop key skills, students must engage in hands-on applied learning projects that nurture the development of three competencies above and beyond core subjects: (a) learning and innovation skills, (b) information, media, and technology skills; and (c) life and career skills (see Figure 2.5).

Learning and innovation skills focus on critical thinking, communication, collaboration, and creativity. Skills in the second category include *information and media literacy skills* and *ICT (information, communications, and technology) skills*. 21st-century professionals thrive by taking advantage of rich informational resources, but we must know how to wade through those resources and make sense of them, filtering out the noise. Finally, *life and career skills* allow students to thrive in a highly competitive and constantly evolving global environment. Career skills were not formerly considered to

Figure 2.5 Core Components of 21st-Century Skills

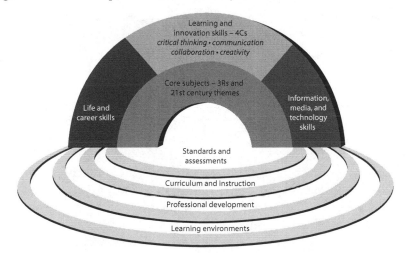

Note. From Partnership for 21st Century Skills (2013). Reproduced with permission.

be within the province of education. Here, 21st-century requirements make them an inherent component of modern education. These skills include flexibility, initiative, cross-cultural understanding, productivity, and leadership.

Examining the 21st-century skills framework, we can see why eService-Learning makes a superb conduit for teaching and nurturing such skills (see Table 2.1). By its very definition, *eService-Learning* requires learning and innovation, because students must think creatively to deliver a product, collaborate with others, and communicate clearly with their peers and the community partner.

eService-Learning also meshes well with the information category, as students must assess and evaluate information to produce for or serve the community partner. They also must apply technology effectively to deliver the product and/or communicate with the community partner in some cases. At its heart, eService-Learning also builds career skills by requiring students to interact effectively with others, manage products or service timelines, and be responsible to others.

In fact, eService-Learning may have a strategic advantage over traditional service-learning as a vehicle for teaching 21st-century skills, precisely *because* of the electronic medium involved. By its very definition, *eService-Learning* will require students to interact with technology in a virtual medium, as opposed to traditional service-learning.

Now let's consider Dr. Johnston's graduate-level marketing course, wherein the students created a stellar marketing plan for the rural nonprofit, enabling the students to hone their professional skills and the nonprofit to receive a great strategy to grow its revenues to help local women. Dr. Johnston challenges her online marketing strategy students to create a top-notch marketing plan for a rural nonprofit that wants to market local women's crafts online. The nonprofit receives a first-rate marketing plan to focus its future sales efforts.

The students gain experience and a deeper understanding of marketing theories. The project refines their learning and innovation skills by requiring critical thinking and problem solving (applying strategic marketing concepts to the women's group) and creativity (developing strategies to meet the needs of the community group). Because they have hands-on experience developing the strategic marketing plan, the students improve their professional skills, and some even choose to feature that experience in their résumé. The electronic medium encourages the students to improve their digital communication skills during the webinars with the community partner and asynchronous communications. Because of that inherent skill husbandry, eService-Learning is indeed an extremely promising delivery mechanism for delivering the 21st-century skills our students need to thrive.

TABLE 2.1
How eService-Learning Fosters 21st-Century Skills

Learning and Innovation	Information Literacy, Media Literacy, and Information, Communications, and Technology	Career and Life
Creativity and innovation • Think creatively • Work creatively with others	Information literacy • Assess and evaluate information • Use and manage information	Flexibility and adaptability • Be flexible
Critical thinking and problem solving • Reason effectively • Use systems thinking • Make judgments and decisions • Solve problems	Media literacy • Create media products	Initiative and self-direction • Manage goals and time • Work independently • Be self-directed learners
Communication and collaboration • Communicate clearly • Collaborate with others	Information, communication, and technology literacy • Apply technology effectively	Social and cross-cultural skills • Interact effectively with others • Work effectively in diverse teams
		Productivity and accountability • Manage projects • Produce results
		Leadership and responsibility • Guide and lead others • Be responsible to others

Indeed, eService-Learning has potential to *outperform* traditional service-learning on several dimensions, such as skill development—a notion that surely will be considered heresy by traditional service-learning adherents. Consider Extreme eService-Learning, where both the service and the instruction occur online. It is true that eService-Learning students may not learn in situ office skills such as office decorum, how to dress, and body language (with one critical exception: they learn to serve the client). For example, Extreme eService-Learning students must hit the proverbial ground running to navigate and negotiate client needs quickly in order to deliver a product. These students ultimately function more as consultants than employees. Extreme eService-Learning strips away the niceties to focus on brass tacks, producing a stellar deliverable (a product for the community partner). With more fields, such as public administration, increasingly relying on privatization and consulting, these consulting skill sets of effectively interacting with clients digitally will serve students well in the 21st-century business and governmental landscape.

Converting a Traditional Service-Learning Course to eService-Learning

Pamela's on-site risk management course always features service-learning. Most recently, Pamela had her students evaluate wheelchair access and other Americans with Disabilities Act (ADA) issues for the local county health clinic. During the first week of class, she takes her class to the clinic, where they embark on a tour and meet in person with the clinic's human resource director. For the next few weeks, students learn the ADA policies and create a template for how to evaluate the facility, particularly focusing on identifying necessary improvements and how they impact risk concerns at the clinic. The students return for field visits several times throughout the course, conducting a careful examination of the facility and taking the opportunity to interview other personnel, such as clinic staff and even patients. At the end of the semester, the human resource director visits the class to hear the student teams present their findings and recommendations.

Because of the shifting needs of the university, Pamela must now teach her risk management course online, with students from all over the country. Even though she has taught the course online numerous times, she has not tried eService-Learning in her online course. Can she successfully transition the service-learning component online? How will students connect to the community partner (the human resources director)? How will they do a thorough evaluation without physically inspecting the clinic? Will they understand local political dynamics and fiscal context enough to develop usable recommendations? Is it possible without a physical connection to the location?

It is indeed possible, with some modification. Pamela teaches the HR director to use Skype and the university's virtual meeting software, and she uses that to introduce the director to the students during a 1-hour webinar.

Pamela develops a brief video with a tour of the facility, showing them some of the ADA-related challenges (this video is posted in the course shell). Instead of doing field visits, Pamela challenges her students to find best practices from other ADA projects and relevant case studies of other hospitals that had undertaken strategic ADA improvements. The students excel at this task, and some even visit their local hospital HR directors to interview them about ADA strategies, broadening the class's collective scope of knowledge. Other students truly take the research challenge to heart, finding not only ADA resources but also culturally sensitive communication strategies, as the HR director mentioned that as an ongoing challenge as well. The students work in teams, with some choosing to create narrated PowerPoint presentations with their recommendations, and others choosing to present live through webinar format to the HR director, who welcomed their astute findings and the wide variety of perspectives they represented.

It is possible, but there are key differences. First, Pamela modified the scope of the project; instead of gaining deep field knowledge of the facility, students had to connect with deep knowledge of the ADA best practices research. Second, Pamela modified the connection modality, connecting the HR director through webinars and Skype rather than through face-to-face meetings. Third, reflections occurred through online blogs rather than through verbal class discussions. Pamela was later pleasantly surprised to learn that several of the online students shared the results of their best practices research with the local hospital administrators in their own communities, resulting in local positive impacts as well. Pamela was pleased by the academic and service outcomes. True enough, the students did not have intimate local knowledge or context, but in lieu of local context, they had literally brought a world of knowledge to bear on the topic through their extensive case research. Practical tips such as those shown in Figure 2.6 may help further ease the path for a first-time eService-Learning practitioner.

Incorporating eService-Learning Into Existing Online Courses

Blake's health literacy course focuses on promoting health literacy to improve patient health outcomes through enhanced communication. His state-of-the-art online course teaches students the importance of clear communication in health care; barriers to clear communication; and the technological, cultural, linguistic, and organizational challenges in creating a culture of stellar communication in health organizations.

As patients immediately forget 40% to 80% of the medical information received during their visit (Kessels, 2003), Blake covers a "teach-back" method each semester, wherein students learn to close the gap between the patient and the health practitioner. This teach-back method prompts the

Figure 2.6 Practical Advice for New eService-Learning Practitioners

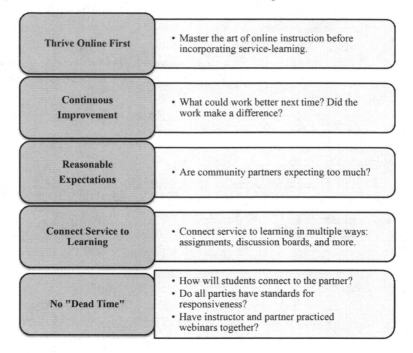

Thrive Online First	• Master the art of online instruction before incorporating service-learning.
Continuous Improvement	• What could work better next time? Did the work make a difference?
Reasonable Expectations	• Are community partners expecting too much?
Connect Service to Learning	• Connect service to learning in multiple ways: assignments, discussion boards, and more.
No "Dead Time"	• How will students connect to the partner? • Do all parties have standards for responsiveness? • Have instructor and partner practiced webinars together?

patients, in an unobtrusive manner, to teach back what instructions they have learned regarding medicines and other requirements to ensure accuracy.

Typically Blake requires his students to practice the methods among themselves. However, intrigued by eService-Learning possibilities, he modifies the assignment so that the students now serve as instructors, teaching rural county health practitioners the method through a combination of video and real-time webinars, then allowing the practitioners to practice teach-back on the students through Skype (as both the instruction and the service occur online, the class becomes an Extreme eService-Learning course). The following semester, he experiments with allowing the online students to conduct the teach-backs at local health clinics in their own communities (a Hybrid I).

Thus, by using this incremental approach, Blake effectively converts his online course into an eService-Learning class by choosing one assignment and fundamentally inverting it so that the instruction services the community in some manner. He experiments over the course of the year, first with the 100% online model and then with a hybrid-based setting, until he discovers the optimal configuration that enhances student learning outcomes and provides strong value to the community partner. For the following year, he redesigns and realigns the course to deepen the connection with his chosen community partner so that all course assignments serve the partner from start to finish. He continues to collect survey, focus group, and interview data from the students and partners (including course evaluations) to ensure that the eService-Learning endeavor adds value for the partner and student learning outcomes.

Institutionalizing eService-Learning

At many colleges, the commitment to service-learning runs deep—through the very veins of the institution itself. How can a college maintain or even strengthen its core commitment to service-learning as its offerings and students increasingly migrate online? Is it possible to honor the values represented by service-learning and continue to foster engaged student-citizens through the online medium?

This question plagues Tracy, the coordinator of the service-learning center at a private midwestern college. Tracy's first and foremost obstacle is sheer cognitive disbelief: Her core service-learning practitioners simply do not believe service-learning can be done online, at least not without significantly compromising quality. Tracy herself is not fully convinced it can be done. She wishes there were more longitudinal studies, hard-core quantitative stuff, that truly validated the learning and engagement benefits of eService-Learning initiatives.

Furthermore, she's concerned about placements. The center's resources are already stretched thin. How will she work with hundreds of community partners instead of the 22 well-established partners in her own community? How will she supervise placements, track service, and ensure the legitimacy of the service? Beyond the quality control challenges, what about risk management? Students may encounter, or create, a liability situation in the service-learning placements resulting from the eService-Learning courses. Moreover, would some programs, such as math or liberal arts, face unique challenges integrating eService-Learning in their online courses?

Beyond the placement logistics, Tracy frets about training (e.g., the technology that service-learning instructors will need to transition online or the training platforms that existing online faculty need to begin incorporating eService-Learning). Tracy also knows she will need significant incentives to encourage and grow eService-Learning, perhaps even incentives that involve altering the sacrosanct tenure and promotion process itself.

Organizationally, eService-Learning may not fit well into the existing mission of her service-learning center, which focuses on local community engagement. A new mission statement, one more globally oriented, would be required—and champions for eService-Learning would need to be cultivated.

Quite literally, a new paradigm would be required to effectively encompass eService-Learning into the mission and structure of the center.

After careful consideration, Tracy decides to make the leap of faith, and she incorporates eService-Learning into the center's strategic plan and updated mission statement. She arranges small seed grants for eService-Learning projects and solicits pioneer faculty to launch the eService-Learning initiative (faculty are selected by a nomination process, making it a position of honor). The inaugural eService-Learning efforts focus on Extreme eService-Learning classes (where both the service and the learning occur entirely online) in order to eliminate placement, risk management measures, or tracking challenges.

Tracy arranges online teaching assistants for the pioneering instructors in the initiative. Working with other departments, she alters the faculty development conference funds to encourage webinar training for instructors interested in eService-Learning training. The instructional design team incorporates eService-Learning into its annual faculty training session and even provides the eService-Learning courses with a separate registration code so that students can easily find the specially designated eService-Learning courses. The chancellor supports the initiative by arranging for a Distinguished Visiting Scholar, one experienced in eService-Learning, to stay in residence at the campus over the summer to mentor faculty who wish to try eService-Learning.

The center's newsletter to all students highlights these eService-Learning showcase courses, with interviews from the pioneering faculty in these efforts (including several courses where faculty paired up to successfully integrate eService-Learning through partner teaching). Pioneering faculty now serve as mentors to future faculty efforts. Finally, Tracy secures a large grant for her college to rigorously study the learning outcomes of the new initiative. The study results persuade the college to further promote the eService-Learning initiative as a way to advance the institution's and the center's mission successfully.

Conclusion

eService-Learning is an extremely promising mechanism for delivering the 21st-century skills our students need to thrive, including information literacy, ICT, innovation, and career skills. Indeed, because of its inherent digital grounding, eService-Learning may ultimately outperform traditional service-learning on some variables such as skill development or even learning outcomes. Thus, far from being a medium of last resort, eService-Learning should be considered a full-bodied service-learning medium in its own right.

Barriers do exist. Established online instructors may not know how to incorporate service-learning into their courses. Experienced traditional service-learning practitioners may not know how to rewire that experience to function effectively online. Most institutions, even those immersed in online learning, have not yet grappled with systematically encouraging eService-Learning in their online offerings. Yet all of those barriers can be overcome.

Without doubt, early innovators in eService-Learning will make mistakes as the nascent medium emerges. Instructors should consider themselves pioneers, forging ahead in a new era of service-learning—with technical, design, and even service mistakes as an integral part of that process. If coupled with careful evaluation of outcomes, experimentation will shape eService-Learning into a powerful new tool to engage new legions of online learners and provide crucial service to nonprofits and other community partners locally and across the globe.

References

Bennett, G., & Green, F. P. (2001). Promoting service-learning via online instruction. *College Student Journal, 35*(4), 491–497.

Bennett, G., Henson, R. K., & Drane, D. (2003). Student experiences with service-learning in sports management. *Journal of Experiential Education, 26*, 61–69.

Blackwell, C. W. (2008). Meeting the objectives of community-based nursing education. In A. Dailey-Hebert, E. Donnelli-Sallee, & L. DiPadova-Stocks (Eds.), *Service-eLearning: Educating for citizenship* (pp. 87–94). Charlotte, NC: Information Age.

Burns, J. M. (1978). *Leadership.* New York, NY: HarperCollins.

Burton, E. (2003). Distance learning and service-learning in the accelerated format. *New Directions for Adult and Continuing Education, 2003*(97), 63–72.

Clayton, P. H., Bringle, R. G., Senor, B., Huq, J., & Morrison, M. (2010). Differentiating and assessing relationships in service-learning and civic engagement: Exploitative, transactional, or transformational. *Michigan Journal of Community Service-Learning, 16*(2), 5–21.

Enos, S., & Morton, K. (2003). Developing a theory and practice of campus community partnerships. In B. Jacoby & Associates (Eds.), *Building partnerships for service-learning* (pp. 20–41). San Francisco, CA: Jossey-Bass.

Eyler, J. S., & Giles, D. E., Jr. (1999). *Where's the learning in service-learning?* San Francisco, CA: Jossey-Bass.

Eyler, J., Giles, D. E., Jr., Stenson, C. M., & Gray, C. J. (2001). *At a glance: What we know about the effects of service-learning on college students, faculty, institutions and communities, 1993–2000* (3rd ed.). Nashville, TN: Vanderbilt University.

Gaytan, J., & McEwen, B. C. (2007). Effective online instructional and assessment strategies. *The American Journal of Distance Education, 2*(3), 117–132.

Guthrie, K. L., & McCracken, H. (2010). Making a difference online: Facilitating service-learning through distance education. *The Internet and Higher Education, 13*(3), 153–157.

Harkavy, I., & Hartley, M. (2010). Pursuing Franklin's dream: Philosophical and historical roots of service-learning. *American Journal of Psychology, 46*(3–4), 418–427.

Hill, J. R., Song, L., & West, R. E. (2009). Social learning theory and web-based learning environments: A review of research and discussion of implications. *The American Journal of Distance Education, 2*(1), 88–103.

Hunter, D. (2007). The virtual student/client experience. *Journal of American Academy of Business, 12*(1), 88–92.

Kessels, R. P. (2003). Patients' memory for medical information. *Journal of the Royal Society of Medicine, 96*(5), 219–222.

Killian, J. (2004). Pedagogical experimentation: Combining traditional, distance, and service-learning techniques. *Journal of Public Affairs Education, 10*(3), 209–224.

Lazar, J., & Preece, J. (1999, December). Implementing service-learning in an online communities course. In *Proceedings of the International Academy for Information Management 1999 conference* (pp. 22–27). Charlotte, NC. Retrieved from http://citeseerx.ist.psu.edu/viewdoc/summary?doi=10.1.1.92.8916

Malvey, D. M., Hamby, E. F., & Fottler, M. D. (2006). E-Service-Learning: A pedagogic innovation for healthcare management education. *Journal of Health Administration Education, 33*(2), 181–198.

Mosley, P. H., & Pennachio, L. (2005). An integration of technology into education majors' civic responsibilities. *Journal of Computing Sciences in Colleges, 20*(3), 121–133.

Muirhead, B. (2004). Encouraging interaction in online courses. *International Journal of Instructional Technology and Distance Learning, 1*(6). Retrieved from http://www.itdl.org/journal/jun_04/article07.htm

National Service-Learning Clearinghouse. (2013). *What is service-learning?* Retrieved from http://www.servicelearning.org/what-is-service-learning

Partnership for 21st Century Skills. (2009). *P2 framework definitions.* Retrieved from http://www.p21.org/storage/documents/P21_Framework_Definitions.pdf

Partnership for 21st Century Skills. (2013). *Framework for 21st century learning.* Retrieved from http://www.p21.org/

Simons, L., & Cleary, B. (2006). The influence of service-learning on students' personal and social development. *College Teaching, 54*(4), 307–320.

Strait, J., & Jones, J. (2009). *Each One, Teach One program.* Retrieved May 20, 2010, from http://www.eric.ed.gov/ERICWebPortal/detail?accno=EJ853211

Strait, J., & Sauer, T. (2004). *Constructing experiential learning for online courses: The birth of e-service.* Retrieved May 20, 2010, from http://www.educause.edu/EDUCAUSE+Quarterly/EDUCAUSEQuarterlyMagazineVolum/ConstructingExperientialLearni/157274

Swan, K. (2002). Building learning communities in online courses: The importance of interaction. *Education, Communication and Information, 2*(1), 23–49.

University of Massachusetts at Amherst Civic Engagement and Service-Learning. (2013). *Core elements of service-learning courses*. Retrieved from http://cesl.umass .edu/core-elements-service-learning-courses

Waldner, L., & Hunter, D. (2008). Client-based courses: Variations in service-learning. *Journal of Public Affairs Education, 14*(2), 219–239.

Waldner, L., McGorry, S., & Widener, M. (2010). Extreme e-service-learning (XES-L): E-service-learning in the 100% online course. *MERLOT Journal of Online Learning and Teaching, 6*(4), 839–851.

Waldner, L., McGorry, S., & Widener, M. (2012). E-service-learning: The evolution of service-learning to engage a growing online student population. *Journal of Higher Education Outreach and Engagement, 16*(2), 123–150.

Waldner, L., Roberts, K., Widener, M., & Sullivan, B. (2011). Serving up justice: Fusing service-learning and social equity in the public administration classroom. *Journal of Public Affairs Education, 17*(2), 209–232.

Wang, W. (2000). Service-learning: Is it good for you? In *American Educational Research Association conference roundtable* (p. 12). New Orleans, LA: American Educational Research Association.

Wilhite, S., & Silver, P. (2005). Educating citizens vs. educating technicians: A false dichotomy for higher education. *National Civic Review, 94*(2), 46–54.

3

DEVELOPING AN eSERVICE-LEARNING EXPERIENCE FOR ONLINE COURSES

Katherine J. Nordyke

There are many factors to be considered when designing an online course, especially one that integrates service-learning. We know and understand what service-learning is and why service-learning promotes and fosters student success and retention, but what to include and how to include service-learning requires some thought, creativity, and often innovation to provide students with the best service-learning experience possible. While not all-inclusive, the following should be considered when developing your course:

- Creating course content (including how service-learning will be integrated based on the selected eService-Learning models identified in chapter 2 of this book)
- Using a virtual classroom to manage the eService-Learning opportunity
- Identifying available course management tools, resources, and software
- Dealing with and managing plagiarism, privacy, and identity issues
- Ensuring Americans with Disabilities Act requirements are met when delivering service-learning in an online presence

- Incorporating professional standards associated with the discipline you are teaching
- Identifying resource levels to assist with online course and eService-Learning development on your campus
- Ensuring that eService-Learning experiences for your students are available through community partners

The focus of this chapter is to examine each of these various elements and how they are present in each of the models of eService-Learning.

Use of Service-Learning in the Online Environment

It would be difficult to dispute the positive impact that service-learning has on students; the benefits service-learning offers communities; and, based on research findings, the overall impact of service-learning on student success and retention. The challenge presents itself, however, in developing experiential service-learning opportunities for students enrolled in online courses. It is important to note, and for faculty to understand, that service-learning is a teaching methodology. With this in mind, how do we begin to develop service-learning for the online environment? Why marry the pedagogies of online learning and service-learning?

In the online environment, learning serves as a facilitator to service-learning, providing the learner with the opportunity to benefit from the service-learning experience just as with those students who engage in service-learning through their seated course. Waldner, McGorry, and Widener (2012) defined *eService-Learning* by stating, "eService-Learning occurs when the instructional component, the service component, or both are conducted online" (p. 125). In their 2008 book, *Service-eLearning: Educating for Citizenship*, Amber Dailey-Hebert, Emily Donnelli Salle, and Laurie N. DiPadova-Stocks described *service-eLearning* (eService-Learning) as "an integrative pedagogy that engages learners through technology in civic inquiry, service, reflection, and action" (p. 125).

David Pratt, associate professor of education and coordinator of learning and technology for Purdue University North Central, acknowledged in the February 2012 issue of *Faculty Focus*, authored by Christopher Hill, that "service learning may be one of the more effective ways of engaging students in the learning process, particularly for the current generation of millennials" and further stated that "it is worth the effort to add a real-world learning experience to a course, and this extends to online courses, where the challenges are even more complex than in a face-to-face course"

(Hill, 2012, p. 1). Service-learning is considered a high-impact program that fosters student success and retention and engages students in direct or indirect opportunities. This holds true for eService-learning as well. Direct service-learning activities refer to face-to-face opportunities with community partners; indirect service-learning includes research-based and advocacy-based activities. Examples of eService-Learning might include the following:

- *A partnership between a course in grant writing and a not-for-profit organization*: The service-learning experience is constructed such that a student might write a grant for a not-for-profit organization,
- *A partnership between an accounting class and a community organization*: A student or student team utilizes their skills and knowledge to provide budget development for the community organization.
- *A partnership between a public administration course and a local community or city government*: Students might provide assistance in developing a community development plan for the community or city.

These eService-Learning opportunities might take place in the community where the student lives, or for a national or global not-for-profit organization. The possibilities are endless and, with geographical boundaries removed, eService-Learning provides students, wherever they reside, the opportunity to engage in service-learning projects on a regional, national, or even global level (Waldner et al., 2012, p. 126).

While academic service-learning linked to courses in the seated classroom environment has been in place for a number of years, the birth of e-service, or eService-Learning, is a relatively new trend. Waldner et al. (2012) shared that online service-learning offerings have not kept tempo with the population of students enrolled in online courses; thus, online learners do not benefit from what service-learning has to offer. Scholars in the field of academic service-learning (Bennett & Green, 2001; Malvey, Hamby & Fottler, 2006; Strait & Hamerlinck, 2010) are embracing this new trend and encourage others in the field of education to find innovative and creative ways to close the gap; integrating service-learning into course content.

Designing the eService-Learning Experience Format

Often we see faculty who are hesitant to combine service-learning as an element of course content because service-learning is most often associated with direct face-to-face interaction. However, this is not necessarily the case.

Service-learning courses offered in both the seated classroom or the online learning environment can be direct, indirect, or a combination of both. As you consider the definition of *service-learning* and your proposed eService-Learning content, it is important to understand that service-learning can take on a wide variety of forms. The form it takes for your students will depend on: (a) the goals and objectives for the course; (b) the issues facing communities—locally, nationally, or globally; and (c) the needs that potential community partners may have identified. In other words, there are many ways for students to experience academic service-learning. Ash and Clayton (2009) share examples of multiple ways in which service-learning can be met; through both indirect and direct service-learning (see Figure 3.1).

Figure 3.1 Course Formats for eService-Learning.

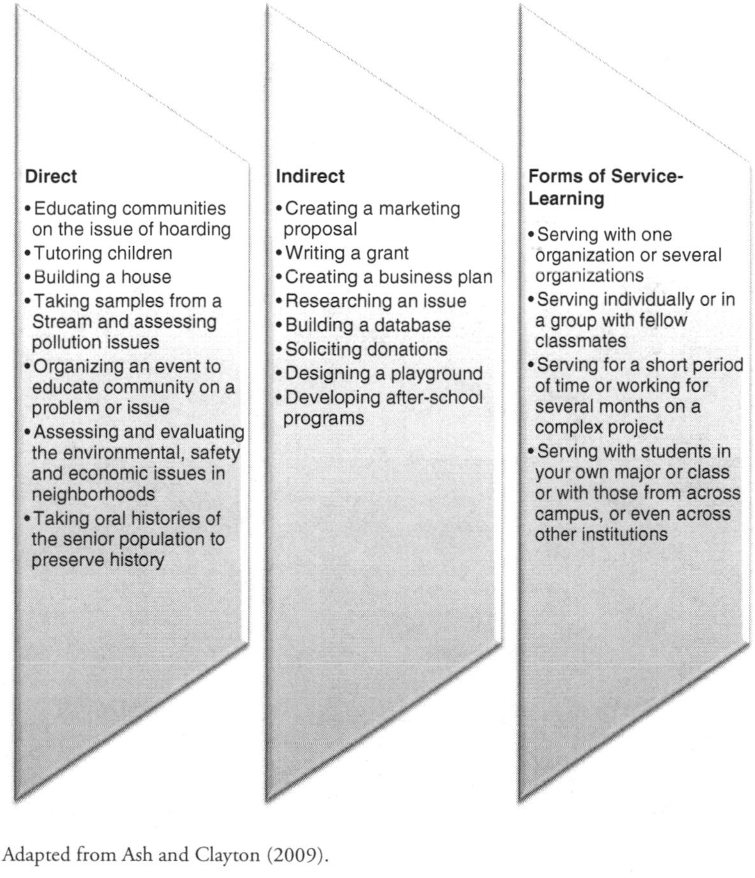

Direct
- Educating communities on the issue of hoarding
- Tutoring children
- Building a house
- Taking samples from a Stream and assessing pollution issues
- Organizing an event to educate community on a problem or issue
- Assessing and evaluating the environmental, safety and economic issues in neighborhoods
- Taking oral histories of the senior population to preserve history

Indirect
- Creating a marketing proposal
- Writing a grant
- Creating a business plan
- Researching an issue
- Building a database
- Soliciting donations
- Designing a playground
- Developing after-school programs

Forms of Service-Learning
- Serving with one organization or several organizations
- Serving individually or in a group with fellow classmates
- Serving for a short period of time or working for several months on a complex project
- Serving with students in your own major or class or with those from across campus, or even across other institutions

Note. Adapted from Ash and Clayton (2009).

Determining the Service-Learning Experience

Now that you have made the commitment to at least consider eService-Learning for your online course, you will also want to consider the most effective way to bring the service-learning experience to your students. Figure 3.2 illustrates the different ways that institutions of higher education generally offer service-learning. Your higher education institution will undoubtedly have guidelines for how service-learning should be structured. Depending on the university, some experiences are offered as an attached component course linked to a designated course, an integrated or embedded element within the course, or as a stand-alone course. Missouri State University, for example, offers service-learning not only as an element embedded within the course, known as integrated service-learning, but also as a one-credit component service-learning course linked to a designated three-credit course. It should be noted that all students enrolled in the one-credit component service-learning course participate in the service-learning experience. Though Missouri State University does not offer service-learning as a stand-alone course, this method may be used within other universities.

Figure 3.2 Missouri State University Methods of Service-Learning Course Delivery

Integrated	Component	Stand-Alone
• Embedded within a course • Students complete 12 to 15 hours of service-learning • All students enrolled in the course are required to complete the service-learning experience • No additional course credit is received • Example: 2-Credit Freshman Seminar course • The course would be listed in the course schedule as a service learning course	• Indepent course linked to a designate course • Students complete 40 hours of service-learning per one credit • Students would enroll in both the Designate Course (3-credit course) and the 1-credit component service-learning course • Example: SWK 250—Interviewing Skills (designate 3-credit course) linked to SWK 300—Social Work Service-Learning (component 1-Credit course) • Both courses would appear on the students' transcript with the 300 Course as the service learning course	• Independent service-learning course • Course is generally associated with an academic major or minor • Variable Credit (generally 1-3 credits depending on the number of service-learning hours; ie: 1=40 hours, 2=80 hours, 3=120 hours) • Example: NUR 456—Service-Learning Field Experience (1–3 credits) • Course would appear on student's transcript as a service-learning course

Note. Figure developed by K. Nordyke.

Service-learning courses, including eService-Learning courses, require all students enrolled in the course to complete a service-learning experience. With the exception of the Missouri State University example described previously and referenced in the previous figure, all other eService-Learning examples described in this chapter are fully integrated into the course and all students enrolled in eService-Learning courses participate.

Once you understand what forms service-learning can take on, and how service-learning can be implemented at your institution, you can begin to develop your eService-Learning course using the checklist found in appendix A. Each of these steps will be discussed in detail within the "Essential Steps for Creating the Course and Syllabus for eService-Learning" section of this chapter.

eService-Learning Program Assessment Tools

When developing service-learning outcomes, the American Association of Community Colleges recommends six elements that should be included in an assessment tool used to evaluate student outcomes for service-learning, including eService-Learning course work (see Figure 3.3).

The American Association of Community Colleges' recommendations are based on the research of Prentice and Robinson (2010). This assessment tool, while it may be adapted to meet the specific needs of college and university service-learning programs, in both the seated and online service-learning environment, is intended to provide educators with a "method to document student learning objectively" (p. 1). To assess these outcomes, Prentice and Robinson developed student and faculty surveys. The Faculty Survey of Course Objectives was developed to measure the degree to which various service-learning outcomes were addressed in the service-learning course (eService-Learning or service-learning in the seated environment). The Student Survey of Course Objectives was developed to measure the degree to which students believed the course addressed various service-learning objectives.

In addition to using surveys or conducting focus groups to assess and evaluate service-learning course outcomes, student reflection rubrics are often used by faculty teaching service-learning courses, including eService-Learning courses, to determine if students are making the connection between their academic course work and their experiential service-learning opportunity with their community partner. Rubrics used for assessing students' critical reflection activities are provided by service-learning organizations such as Campus Compact and by scholars in the field of service-learning who focus their research on critical reflection.

Figure 3.3 Elements for Assessment in Course Outcomes for eService-Learning

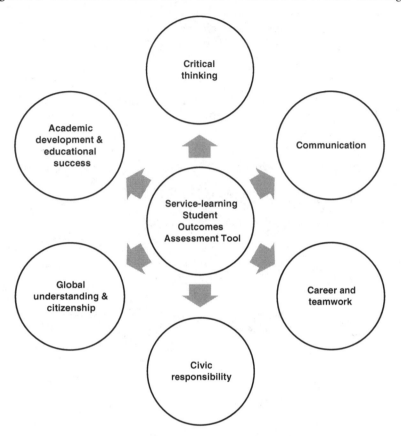

Note. Figure developed by K. Nordyke. Based on the American Association of Community Colleges Recommended Elements for Assessment identified by Prentice and Robinson (2010).

Essential Steps for Creating the Course and Syllabus for eService-Learning

There are several steps necessary in developing your course and the associated syllabi for including service-learning. The identified steps pertain to all aspects of service-learning course development; however, variations may be necessary in formatting the course depending on the type of eService-Learning (Traditional Service-Learning; Hybrid I; Hybrid II; Hybrid III; Extreme eService-Learning) selected. As noted previously, a checklist for the Essential Steps for Creating the Course and Syllabus for eService-Learning is located in appendix A of this chapter; however, details for each of those steps follows.

For step one, you will need to determine how the course is intended to be delivered. Will the instruction be online and the service on-site (Hybrid I)? Will the instruction be on-site and the service online (Hybrid II)? Will the course be a blended course where the instruction and the service are both online and on-site (Hybrid III)? Will the course offer Extreme eService-Learning where both the course and the service are offered online? Once you determine your delivery method you can move forward with further developing your course. (Traditional service-learning is not referenced here as this type of service-learning involves both the course instruction and the service-learning experience on-site.)

For step two, examine the course goals and objectives along with the course's service-learning outcomes and goals. If you are creating a new course, the most important part of this step is to determine the goals and objectives for the course. Consider what skills and abilities you want your students to achieve and determine how students might apply those skills and abilities to engage in community-based problem solving or addressing social justice issues. If the course has previously been created, but you have determined that you want to utilize service-learning as your preferred teaching methodology, you will want to examine how the experiential learning experience of service-learning fits and addresses the predetermined goals and objectives for the course. As you consider a best-fit service-learning opportunity for your students, take into consideration the needs of the community partners and how the course content can assist in addressing the problems or issues they have identified.

For step three, select the community partner(s). You will want to consider how your students can meet the community partners' needs as well as how the course content and the knowledge your students will bring to the table will work in a reciprocal manner. Examples of eService-Learning courses that meet community partner needs might include:

- eService-Learning Marketing: A course that works with a community partner such as the American Heart Association to develop a campaign to reduce smoking among high school students.
- eService-Learning Social Media: A course that works with a community partner such as Global Citizen where students would engage in advocacy and awareness campaigns through the use of social media applications.

As you consider which community partners to select, you will need to consider what you want students to gain from the experiential learning experience and how students can assist community partners in meeting their goals. Additionally, you will need to determine if you will secure the community partners for the students or if the students will be expected to secure their own community partners. A great resource for faculty is to work with your campus service-learning department; service-learning departments generally house a database of community partners with information that includes the types of service-learning projects available and if those projects can be completed in the online environment.

For step four, identify the number of required eService-Learning hours. The number of required service-learning hours is usually determined by institutional guidelines, the Faculty Senate, a department, or an individual instructor. However, make sure that you check any state requirements for service-learning hours. For example, the Missouri Department of Higher Education (2013) requires a minimum of 15 hours of service to qualify as a service-learning experience for credit; this includes traditional service-learning as well as all forms of eService-Learning. Understanding the required number of hours of the eService-Learning experience will assist you in developing the expectations for your students. It is important to ensure that both the student and the community partner understand "how many" service-learning hours are required.

For step five, determine the geographic locations of and implications on potential students and community partners. With an online course, it is somewhat difficult to determine this in advance and is often unknown to the instructor until the course begins and initial contact is made with the students. Determine, in advance, if you will allow students to complete either direct or indirect service-learning for your eService-Learning course. Allowing for flexibility when determining if service-learning opportunities can be direct or indirect is an important consideration; many students live in rural areas and may not have access to physical community partners located in their geographic area. Students in these demographic areas can have a great service-learning experience and make a difference in a community by completing an indirect project.

For step six, assess and evavulate any course management tools (hardware and software) that are available to you. This includes available learning management system software and institutional resources that can assist you in course development and delivery of your course content. You will have to choose which items match the needs of your eService-Learning course. Many colleges and universities offer Faculty Centers for Teaching and Learning; this type of resource center can assist you in developing your course by identifying institution-specific learning management systems such as Blackboard or Canvas and associated tools within the learning management systems (wikis, portfolios, discussion boards, journals, grade administration, assignment posts, blogging, team/group projects, etc.). Additionally, consider what hardware and software computer requirements will be necessary for the course; this is important information to include in your syllabus so that students understand necessary computer requirements (hardware and software) to complete the course. In addition to working with centers for teaching and learning, many colleges and universities have service-learning offices that can provide additional resources and examples of service-learning experiences. Great resources are also available online through Campus Compact.

Keep in mind that quality service-learning experiences require an associated reflection whereby the student analyzes the service-learning experience and synthesizes the information gained. The reflection assignment can take on one or more forms such as journals, ePortfolios, blogs, PowerPoint presentations, poster presentations, and so on. Finally, be sure to provide a list of potential community partners that includes contact times and opportunities for interactions (face-to-face, Skype, phone, etc.) along with the required number of hours to complete the service-learning project.

For step seven, assess and evaluate the final product for student conduct, liability, and Americans with Disabilities Act requirements. To address issues of plagiarism you might have students complete your institution's academic integrity and plagiarism requirements. Most colleges and universities that offer any type of online course have some type of online academic integrity tutorial unit that students must complete prior to the start of the course. Having students complete this activity provides them with insight about plagiarism and associated expectations. When developing reflection assignments, consider assignments that focus on critical thinking and encourage completion of ePortfolios, PowerPoint presentations, blogs, YouTube videos, and so on that depict their experience; allowing students to use creative and innovative ways to showcase what they have done and how their experience ties to their course content and the skills, knowledge, and abilities they have acquired. Additionally, allowing students to create ePortfolios as their reflection activity provides a meaningful way for students to write about their eService-Learning experience and provides them with a tool they can use when applying, as an example, for jobs and scholarships.

This step also includes addressing privacy, confidentiality, student conduct, and liability. Consider developing a Confidentiality, Conduct, and Liability Release form. An example of the form used by Missouri State University can be found in appendix B of this chapter. At Missouri State University, students can complete the form in the online environment and submit it to the campus service-learning office; this method provides a record, via electronic signature, that they understand and will comply with items set forth in the form. This is also a great place to include a photo release. It should be noted that if pictures are taken that involve students engaged with clients during the students' service-learning experience, a photo release for any subject should be signed before printing in any publication. You could also place a similar form within your learning management system, ask the students to complete it, scan it, and forward it to you via e-mail.

You will also want to ensure that your course meets any Americans with Disabilities Act requirements, including the student's service-learning experience. For example, a wheelchair bound student needs a community-partner that provides on-site ramps, elevators, and so on, or would agree to the student completing the assigned service-learning project in his or her own environment. In this case, service-learning might take the form of developing educational content for kindergarten to third-grade students focusing on "going green" projects; the student, if an education major, for example, could develop the content within his or her own living environment.

For step eight, identify professional standards required for the course or the service-learning experience. For example, what professional standards are required for those pursuing a career in accounting? You will want to ensure that the service-learning experience allows students to meet any necessary standards. If the eService-Learning course involves working with special needs children, then the student, as a part of their service-learning experience, might need to develop lesson plans or create educational activities for after-school programming. When considering standards, also check your state's service-learning standards; understanding any professional or state standards prior to developing your course and associated syllabus is beneficial.

For step nine, review what you have created for academic rigor, reflection activities, and grading criteria. As you develop or revise your existing course syllabus, consider the important elements shown in Figure 3.4. and appendices A and D. You will want to ensure the course and the associated service-learning experience is academically rigorous; this applies to both direct and indirect service-learning. Also, identify the course goals and objectives and identify how students will be graded for their service-learning activity. Students should be evaluated according to their effectiveness in integrating any course materials, skills, and knowledge into the service-learning activity; the grade should not be based on completion of the required service-learning experience, but rather on course reflection work that ties the course content to their eService-Learning experience.

Appendix C is an example of an eService-Learning paragraph that could be included in your syllabus, and appendix D is a checklist of core elements required for eService-Learning courses. The paragraph and core elements

Figure 3.4 Missouri State University CASL Core Syllabus Elements for Service-Learning

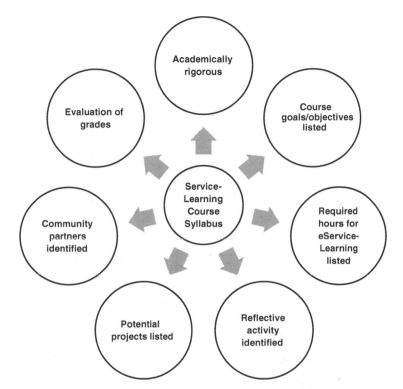

Note. Developed by K. Nordyke. Based on CASL Core Elements required for service-learning courses at Missouri State University as determined by the MSU Faculty Senate Oversight Committee. For more information see www.missouristate.edu/casl

were developed by the Missouri State University Faculty Senate Oversight Committee in conjunction with the Missouri State University Office of Citizenship and Service-Learning and can assist you in developing your course and your course syllabus (Office of Citizenship and Service-Learning [CASL], 2013). Extended examples of each kind of eService-Learning can be found in chapters 5 through 9 of this text.

Final Thoughts on the Essential Steps

Deciding to include eService-Learning in your online course curriculum might seem overwhelming, and creating a syllabus to support the eService-Learning course structure can often be a daunting task; however, if your goal is to move your course to student-centered 21st-century learning, consider making your online course an eService-Learning course. The nine steps provided in this chapter can assist you in your eService-Learning course development and syllabus creation. Engaging your students in eService-Learning will not only enhance your course offering but also provide your students with a meaningful experience—connecting the classroom to the real-world—and help them develop the essential skills they will need to be successful in a global environment.

References

Ash, S. L., & Clayton, P. H. (2009). *Learning through critical reflection: A tutorial for service-learning students* (Instructor version). Raleigh, NC: Authors.

Bennett, G., & Green, F. P. (2001). Promoting service learning via online instruction. *College Student Journal, 35*(4), 491–498.

Dailey-Hebert, A., Salle, E. D., & DiPadova-Stocks, L. N. (2008). *Service-elearning: Educating for Citizenship*. Charlotte, NC: Information Age.

Hill, C. (2012). Four keys to successful service learning in online courses. *Faculty Focus: Distance Education Report, 14*(24), 1–5.

Malvey, D. M., Hamby, E. F., & Fottler, M. D. (2006). E-service learning: A pedagogic innovation for healthcare management education. *Journal of Health Administration Education, 23*(2), 181–98.

Missouri Department of Higher Education. (2013). *MDHE performance indicators survey*. Retrieved January 30, 2015 from dhe.mo.gov/documents/DHE-PIS2013. xlsx

Office of Citizenship and Service-Learning (CASL). 2013. *Missouri State University.* Retrieved from http://missouristate.edu/casl.

Prentice, M., & Robinson, G. (2010). *Improving student learning outcomes with service learning*. Washington, DC: American Association of Community Colleges.

Strait, J., & Hamerlinck, J. (2010). *Service-learning in online courses webinar*. Retrieved September 23, 2013 from Center for Digital Civic Engagement website: http://cdce.wordpress.com/2010/02/10/service-learning-in-online-courses-webinar/

Waldner, L. S., McGorry, S. Y. & Widener, M. C. (2012). E-service-Learning: The evolution of service-learning to engage a growing online student population. *Journal of Higher Education Outreach and Engagement, 16*(2), 123–150.

APPENDIX A: ESSENTIAL STEPS FOR CREATING THE COURSE AND SYLLABUS FOR eSERVICE-LEARNING

- ☐ Step 1: Determine course delivery
- ☐ Step 2: Determine course goals, skills, and abilities
- ☐ Step 3: Select community partners
- ☐ Step 4: Identify the number of required eService-Learning hours
- ☐ Step 5: Determine geographic locations and implications
- ☐ Step 6: Assess and evaluate course management tools
- ☐ Step 7: Assess and evaluate the final product for student conduct, liability, and ADA requirements
- ☐ Step 8: Identify professional standards for the course
- ☐ Step 9: Review for academic rigor, reflection activities, and grading criteria

---

These essential steps for creating the course and syllabus can be applied to both Traditional Service-Learning and eService-Learning.

APPENDIX B: SAMPLE CONFIDENTIALITY, CONDUCT, LIABILITY, PHOTO, AND PUBLICATION RELEASE FORM

CASL Student Permission and Release Form

First Name: Last Name:

M#:   Semester: Year:

Course Number: Instructor:

CONFIDENTIALITY, CONDUCT, AND LIABILITY RELEASE

☐ **By checking this box I acknowledge that I have read and understand the following paragraphs regarding confidentiality, conduct, and liability.**

CONFIDENTIALITY

As a part of the service-learning course experience, you may share in privileged information. You may learn information about clients or patients that is covered by rules of confidentiality. Speak to your supervisor to discuss how the obligations of confidentiality may apply to you. Do not reveal or discuss information about clients or patients without permission of the professionals for whom you are working.

CONDUCT

You are expected to maintain professional conduct at all times as you are not only representing yourself, but representing Missouri State University as well. Additionally, should you observe or hear of activities that are legally or morally questionable, you have a responsibility to report those activities to your community partner supervisor, the CASL office, and your course instructor.

LIABILITY

You acknowledge that student health insurance may be purchased and that you can contact Taylor Health for additional information. Some community partners may require a student to carry liability insurance. If liability insurance is required, your community partners, the Office of Citizenship and Service-Learning, or your instructor will advise you. If you are conducting research with human subjects, the Missouri State University requires certain guidelines to be met. Please contact your instructor for the requirements pertaining to research.

PHOTOGRAPHIC RELEASE (CHECK ONLY ONE BOX)

☐ I certify that I have read the following Photographic Release Statement and hereby give my permission to be photographed as a part of my service-learning course experience.

☐ I certify that I have read the following Photographic Release Statement and DO NOT give my permission to be photographed as a part of my service-learning course experience.

I hereby irrevocably consent to and authorize Missouri State University, its officers, and employees, ("University") the use of my image, voice, and/or likeness as follows: The University shall have the right to photograph, publish, republish, adapt, exhibit, perform, reproduce, edit, modify, make derivative works, distribute, display, or otherwise use or reuse my image, voice and/or likeness in connection with any product of service in all markets, media, or technology now known or hereafter developed in University products or services, as long as there is no intent to use the image, voice, and/or likeness in a disparaging manner. University may exercise any of these rights itself or through any successors, transferees, licensees, distributors, or other parties, commercial or nonprofit. I acknowledge receipt of good and valuable consideration in exchange for this Release, which may simply be the opportunity to present the University in its promotional and advertising materials as described previously.

PUBLICATION PERMISSION (CHECK ONLY ONE BOX)

☐ I certify that I have read the following Publication Release Statement and hereby give my permission to copy, print, or distribute my service-learning reflection assignment and/or evaluation comments.

☐ I certify that I have read the following Publication Release Statement and DO NOT give my permission to copy, print, or distribute my service-learning reflection assignment and/or evaluation comments.

I hereby grant Missouri State University permission to copy, print, and distribute my service-learning reflection assignment and/or evaluation comments (the "work") and to incorporate the work, in whole or in part, into the Citizenship and Service-learning ("CASL") Annual Report, website, programs, and/or any other promotional materials. I grant Missouri State University the right to edit the work for spelling, grammatical, or sentence structure errors.

The sample Confidentiality, Conduct, Liability, Photo, and Publication Release Form can be utilized for both Traditional Service-Learning and eService-Learning.

APPENDIX C: SAMPLE SERVICE-LEARNING PARAGRAPH

Service-Learning Course Statement

Service-Learning that incorporates a community service experience with classroom instruction has been integrated into this course to provide a community-based learning experience. Service-Learning addresses the practice of citizenship and promotes an awareness of and participation in public affairs. The Service-Learning course requires a minimum of ___ hours of unpaid service to a not-for-profit community organization, government agency or public service provider. The community partner(s) for this course is/are _____ and/or others as approved by the Service-Learning office and course instructor. The community service placement will relate to the course learning objectives as outlined in this syllabus. Reflection assignments are assigned to help students understand discipline concepts and develop higher-order critical thinking skills. Additionally, this course provides students with real world experience that can be included on resumes; offers the ability to test career choices, to apply theories and concepts learned in class and make connections to the real world; and offers the opportunity to have a positive impact in our community. To assess the integration of the Service-Learning portion of this course, an assessment during the last three weeks of the semester will be administered (either online or in person). The evaluation results will assist the instructor in the further development of this course, especially as it relates to the Service-Learning project. Results are provided to the instructor after the grades are submitted to the Registrar's Office.

The sample Service-Learning Paragraph can be adapted to fit both Traditional Service-Learning and eService-Learning for inclusion in course syllabi.

APPENDIX D: CORE ELEMENT CHECKLIST FOR SERVICE-LEARNING COURSES

Core Element Checklist for Service-Learning Courses

To be designated as a **Service-Learning (SL)** course in the Missouri State University course schedule and for all administrative purposes, the following criteria must be met.

☐ 1. The Service-Learning project is <u>academically rigorous</u>, as determined by Department and Curriculum committees, and appropriate for the students' academic preparation and course content.

☐ 2. The course is arranged in partnership with an <u>approved</u> community partner(s). Faculty has identified potential community partner(s) that are appropriate for the course being taught.

☐ 3. The experience provides the community partner(s) with <u>useful service</u> (i.e., tutoring, enrichment lessons, health education, research, report writing) as distinct from mere observation. Give examples of the projects that will be undertaken.

☐ 4. The Service-Learning project/activity must require at least <u>15 hours</u> of unpaid out-of-class service, including appropriate contact time and opportunities for interaction with the Community Partner.

☐ 5. The Service-Learning project/activity <u>must constitute a minimum of 15% of the student's grade</u>.

☐ 6. Students are evaluated according to their <u>effectiveness in integrating course material and the community service activity</u>, not just for completing the required service.

☐ 7. The course assignments include a <u>reflective exercise</u> that requires students to analyze the eService-Learning experiences and synthesize information gained that enriches their academic studies. Readings, writing assignments, journaling, and project assignments are designed to accommodate and integrate the civic engagement component of the course.

☐ 8. Students will be given an instrument to assess the integrated Service-Learning project and its integration into the course.

☐ 9. The partnership does not appear to represent a conflict of interest to the faculty or students participating in the Service-Learning experience.

The Core Element Checklist can be applied to both Traditional Service-Learning and eService-Learning courses.

4

SUPPORTING eSERVICE-LEARNING THROUGH TECHNOLOGY

Jean Strait

The rapid improvement of technology is changing the face of education. If educators and schools are to foster meaningful learning, then the ways that we use technologies in schools must change from technology-as-teacher to technology-as-partner in the learning process (Jonassen, Howland, Marra, & Crismond, 2008). Technology isn't just the hardware and applications teachers and students have, it is also the instruction, environment, and implementation strategies that teachers create and use to engage students in the learning process. Jonassen et al. called these technologies *learning technologies*, which are defined as any activities that engage learners in "active, constructive, intentional, authentic, and cooperative learning."

I began my teaching career over 30 years ago, and I had what would have been considered an education technology class. It consisted of learning how to use an overhead projector, an opaque projector, and a spirit master copier. These copiers used carbon paper and would make purple copies of everything. Computers were something only NASA had. No one had any idea we'd have an Internet that would bring us any information we wanted within an instant. When I share this with my students, the first thing they ask me, after making some kind of "Dr. J you're old" comment, is, "What do you think will happen in the next 30 years?" I can't wait to find out. I believe we always will have incredible tools, but I continually remind my students that it's the teacher who makes or breaks any tool. If a teacher doesn't like a tool or isn't comfortable with it, the students won't use it either. I also stress that teachers have to stay current on the latest technologies and applications as part of their professional development and practice.

Technologies support meaningful learning when they fulfill a learning need—when interactions with technologies are learner initiated and learner controlled and when interactions with the technologies are conceptually and intellectually engaging. Technologies should function as intellectual tool kits that enable learners to build more meaningful personal interpretations and representations of the world.

How Technologies Foster Learning

Educators continue to use technology to teach as they have been teaching, as purveyors of information and knowledge. For the past 20 years, communication and multimedia tools have dominated technology. We can produce great works, but what has the student learned as a result of using that technology? In today's world, technologies should be used as engagers and facilitators of thinking. But to learn with various technologies, we need to reframe what we believe technology is and how it can function.

Jonassen and Reeves (1996) suggested the following guidelines for learning with technology. Technology should be used

- as a tool to support knowledge construction,
- as a vehicle for exploring knowledge to support learning,
- as an authentic context to support learning by doing,
- as a social medium to support learning by conversing, and
- as an intellectual partner to support learning by reflecting.

I believe educators currently do the first two quite well, but most have stopped there. What if educators started using technology for other learning purposes? What would it look like to use virtual reality as a simulation for future career training, or what would a controllable problem space for student brainstorming look like? How could social media be used to solve a community problem by bringing the best minds together to create the solution? The key ingredient for each is that technologies foster learning *when they fulfill a learning need.*

According to Jonassen et al. (2008), technology can be used to support knowledge construction, to explore and support learning, and, for analysis, to break learning apart and reflect on the components. Learners and technologies are partners, working together to facilitate meaning.

Faculty and administrators often express the anxiety they have experienced at one time or another about selecting and using technology. Higher education institutions are behind in faculty development to train staff in the use of new technologies and how to incorporate them into teaching. Many times, online classes become a visual lecture. Students need interaction for engagement. There are three major steps every faculty and administrator should be able to take. These include using technology to extend instructional impact, developing an online community or virtual culture, and teaching technology to students. The new role for faculty and administrators will be to operate as mediators of the learner-technology partnership.

Step 1: Using Technology to Extend Instructional Impact

I have to admit that much of the emerging technology sounds really exciting to me. I want to try out everything, and yet I have time for nothing. When experimenting with that new bell or whistle, faculty must look for the end result. What is the instructional impact? For example, when planning for my students' eService-Learning, I have to consider what technology they will have on hand, what the university can provide, and what I have that they can use. When we first started Each One, Teach One at Hamline, we had only the use of a password-protected course shell in Blackboard software. We chose it because we wanted to provide a secure platform for the middle school students. It was slow but did the job of distance learning. Today, my students use cell phones and tablets to do the same work. This equipment is faster, and the technology is better. Considering our end goal—to be effective tutors and mentors—we need a fast response system that is inexpensive and easy to use. In addition, the vast amount of resources and relationships available online challenges educators to not only rethink their roles and responsibilities but also show their students how to filter information.

Step 2: Developing an Online Community and Virtual Culture

When I first started teaching online, I remember how hard it was to make connections to students. Everything I said had to be typed, and students couldn't read my tone or my gestures. As my teaching evolved, I became increasingly sensitive to my wording in written communication, and I made a commitment to respond to each student in the class at least once a day. I tried to build in components for the class where students felt comfortable and were able to ask questions and be respectful to one another. This level of planning and implementation takes a great deal of time. It became easier with each online class I taught, as students would know my expectations and could help students who were new to my teaching style. They would hold each other accountable for the work that needed to be done. A positive virtual culture is essential for the success of any eService-Learning project. Teachers need to build a strong community foundation, or it may be difficult to recraft the culture later. Be clear with expectations and address them at the very start of a course. It is easy to make assumptions in an online environment that can break down trust and communication. One of the best pieces of advice I can give is to not try to do everything at once. Just pick one idea you want to work on and then build it to success.

Step 3: Teaching Technology to Students

It's common to hear stories about students teaching teachers how to use some tool or device on the computer. Young students don't have the fear of breaking something like many of us older professors do. However, if I'm unfamiliar with a particular technology that I want to use in a course, I make sure to not only learn how to use it but also learn how to teach my students how to use it. Often, my students have other ways of using the technology and show me their shortcuts. As a digital immigrant (or one who was not born using technology like my digital native students), I welcome the reciprocity in the teaching process. I build relational trust every time I have my students teach me something and I use it in class. I also let the students help choose the technology that will be used and keep a running list of websites, tools, and strategies that my students can access and add to for future students.

Using Technology in Service-Learning

Most traditional face-to-face classes have some kind of technology component. It might be readings on a website or from an e-book, viewings of YouTube videos, or discussions on a commercial premade course shell. Whatever the choice, the technology is used to supplement the traditional instruction. In online courses, technology is the means of communication for the entire course. Hybrid classes fall in between these two and, depending on the purpose of the course, the technology, applications, and instructional delivery can vary dramatically. People expect to work, learn, and study wherever and whenever they want. Twenty-first-century skills build the competencies for work and play beyond the classroom. Telecommuting is on the rise for many businesses. Digital media literacy continues to rise in level of importance as a major career skill in every discipline and every profession.

TABLE 4.1
Service-Learning Activities and Technology Usage

Service-Learning Task or Activity	*Example of Technology*
Program management	Databases and course platforms
Community partner participation	Communication, discussion boards
Curricular tools	Blackboard course platform, books
Community service	Posting on websites, communication
Reflection	Discussion boards, group work
Program evaluation	Online or paper evaluation

Seifer and Mihalynuk (2003) suggested uses of technology in service-learning projects and classes for traditional service-learning, where both the instruction and the service are done face-to-face. Table 4.1 provides examples of each.

In the past five years, the majority of research done on educational technology has centered on learning and technical support. As teachers' practice and pedagogy emerge around eService-Learning, educators will need to look beyond the managerial and programmatic tasks that technology currently performs and utilize tools for higher level thinking and learning. While technology may look "cool," teachers need to focus on *what* they need to teach and *how* they plan to teach it. In other words, the technology used in an eService-Learning course needs to align with the pedagogical goals of the course.

Matching Technology Tools and eService-Learning

As educators experiment with the different types of service-learning (Waldner, McGorry, & Widener, 2012), and as more mobile applications become available each day, teachers are starting to see new uses for technology in eService-Learning. Course and service delivery, communication, data collection and analysis, and reflection are the components of eService-Learning. Table 4.2 suggests examples of new hardware technologies and applications (Edudemic, 2013) teachers can experiment with when using a specific type of service-learning.

Take a minute to examine Table 4.2. How many of these technologies are new to you? Service-learning directors could generate a newsletter or training around one or two new tools each semester and keep a database of tools that work well for certain classes, content areas, or eService-Learning hybrid types, which can be shared as an online resource.

TABLE 4.2
Technology Use in the Stages of eService-Learning

Stages of the eService-Learning Process	Hardware	Software or Function
1. Content delivery	Desktop computer, laptop, netbook, and tablet	Videos, e-books, YouTube, Internet, Blackboard, podcasts
2. Service delivery	Phone, desktop computer, laptop, netbook, and tablet	Creating digital media products for community partner
3. Communication	Phone, netbook, and tablet	E-mail, texting, videoconferencing
4. Data collection	Phone, camera, netbook, and tablet	Online survey, mapping software, public surveys
5. Data analysis	Phone, camera, netbook, and tablet	SPSS, free/open software applications
6. Participant reflection	Phone, netbook, and tablet	Written journals, blogs, videos, podcasts

Content Delivery

Content delivery for any type of eService-Learning can be provided through videos, e-books, Internet tools, and podcasts. If you are new to eService-Learning, consider what the course and service goals are—then choose what tools will best help you meet those goals. For example, as a teacher-educator, I use a Blackboard course platform that houses all of my university's online courses. This is a shell that students can enter through and engage in all class functions. I often post videos, YouTube links, and current news articles in my course platform for use during class discussions. In turn, I have an area where students can post these same kinds of tools to share with their course peers and me.

Service Delivery

Once you have constructed your content area, as an instructor, you need to construct your service delivery. Depending on the type of eService-Learning hybrid being used for your class, students could provide live one-on-one tutoring, create a digital media product for a client, or collect data for a nonprofit. Each one of these would require a slightly different configuration. Students providing tutoring will need resources to assist those they tutor, some kind of link or connection to communicate with the community partner about the person tutored, and some way to interact with the tutee to provide the service needed, along with a schedule and format for providing that service.

Communication

I have found the best way to structure communication is to address the content and service goals. I need to be sure that the community partner has a way to communicate with my students and me, and we can all communicate with each other. Traditionally, we use phones and e-mail, but I am finding that the use of videoconferencing during class time is very valuable. Recently, I team taught with a colleague from the East Coast using a feature in Blackboard known as Blackboard Collaborate. My colleague and I both signed into Blackboard Collaborate and projected visuals of both classes and us. I believe this could also be used with community partner engagement. Colleges and universities will have to serve as a host, setting up the collaborative space so that the community partners can assess it from their workspace or place of business.

Technology for Data Collection and Analysis

Service-learning practitioners have already been using technology for content delivery, service delivery, and communication in face-to-face classes. However, tools for data collection, data analysis, and reflection have lagged behind in development. Here are two simple tools that can be implemented in eService-Learning relatively quickly and are free to use.

Data collection: Open Data Kit (ODK) is a free and open-source set of tools that help organizations author, field, and manage mobile data collection solutions. ODK provides an out-of-the-box solution for users to

- build a data collection form or survey,
- collect the data on a mobile device and send it to a server, and
- aggregate the collected data on a server and extract it in useful formats.

In addition to socioeconomic and health surveys with GPS locations and images, ODK is being used to create decision support for clinicians and for building multimedia-rich nature mapping tools.

Data analysis: QDA (Qualitative Data Analysis) Miner Lite is a free and easy-to-use version of popular computer-assisted qualitative analysis software. It can be used for the analysis of textual data such as interview and news transcripts and open-ended responses, as well as for the analysis of still images. (See more at http://provalisresearch.com/products/qualitative-data-analysis-software/freeware/#sthash.wEjf9xPx.dpuf)

Tools for the Reflection Process

Podcasting is a great way to send discussions, talks, and dialogs to many different platforms globally. *Google Docs* is a format used by many students and teachers to share data so that they can be edited and revised, no printing required. *iPads* are a great way to capture spontaneous video that is easily uploaded to a course format.

Do you have some ideas of tools you like to use? The possibilities and combinations are limitless. I encourage you to contact us and let us know what you are trying or using so we can add it to our database of current practices. As of the publication of this text, our team was the only group looking at ways to use technology in eService-Learning, and we welcome any examples and ideas you'd like to share with us.

Conclusion

Educators rely on tools to teach concepts. As technology evolves so do the tools we use to educate. But technology does not teach or convey meaning to students. It is no more than a software program or an app. Without the optimized learning environment and pedagogical expert to engage students, technology cannot be optimized. It might look good, it might sound good, but unless we ask what learning need it fulfills and can answer in meaningful context, we shouldn't use a technology just because it's there. You wouldn't use a screwdriver to hammer in a nail when you have a hammer to use. But if technology can provide an easier, more efficient way to fulfill a learning need (i.e., using a nail gun), educators should be open to trying it and allowing students to benefit from its use.

Teachers must strive to move out of the digital immigrant mold. Nine out of 10 higher education students have a cell phone and tablet to access information. We should be teaching them the best ways to access and use this data. eService-Learning is the perfect arena for educators and students to do just that.

References

Edudemic. (2013). *50 technology tools every teacher should know about.* Retrieved September 28, 2013, from www.Edudemic.com/50-Education-Technology-Tools-Every-Teacher-Should-know-about/

Jonassen, D., Howland, J., Marra, R. M., & Crismond, D. (2008). *Meaningful learning with technology.* Portsmouth, NH: Heinemann.

Jonassen, D. H., & Reeves, T. C. (1996). Learning with technology: Using computers as cognitive tools. In D. Jonassen (Ed.), *Handbook of research on education
communications and technology* (pp. 693–719). New York, NY: Macmillian.

Seifer, S. D., & Mihalynuk, T. V. (2003). *The use of technology in higher education:
Service-learning partnerships for health*. Retrieved October 26, 2013, from the
National Service-Learning Clearinghouse.

Waldner, L. S., McGorry, S. Y., & Widener, M. C. (2012). E-service-learning: The
evolution of service-learning to engage a growing online student population.
Journal of Higher Education Outreach and Engagement, 16(2), 123–150.

PART TWO

MODELS FOR eSERVICE-LEARNING

HYBRID I

Missouri State University Embraces eService-Learning

Katherine J. Nordyke

Missouri State University is located in Springfield, Missouri, and supports six academic colleges, a graduate college, and the William H. Darr School of Agriculture. The university employs some 4,000 faculty and staff, with 90% of the full-time faculty having the most advanced degrees available in their field. Missouri State University competes in the NCAA Division I athletics program and receives millions of dollars in grants each year for research. In addition to the programs offered on the Springfield, Missouri, campus, Missouri State University has three additional campuses including one campus in Dalian, China. Missouri State University prides itself on being a global campus where in the fall of 2010 more than 1,500 students from other countries were enrolled on the Springfield campus, and where hundreds of students participate in study-away programs each year (Missouri State University, 2010).

In 1995, the Missouri General Assembly gave Missouri State University its public affairs mission as reflected in the university's Mission Statement (Missouri State University, n.d.), which states:

> Missouri State University is a public, comprehensive metropolitan system with a statewide mission in public affairs, whose purpose is to develop education persons. The University's identity is distinguished by this public

affairs mission, which entails a campus-wide commitment to foster competence and responsibility in ethical leadership, cultural competence and community engagement.

The academic experience is grounded in a general education curriculum which draws heavily from the liberal arts and sciences. This foundation provides the basis for mastery of disciplinary and professional studies. It also provides essential forums in which students develop the capacity to make well-informed, independent critical judgments about the cultures, values, and institutions in society.

The Missouri State University campuses are structured to address the special needs of the urban and rural populations they serve.

The public affairs mission contains three components (ethical leadership, cultural competence, and community engagement), and hosts a Public Affairs Week and Public Affairs Conference each year. Missouri State University defines the three public affairs components as follows

- **Ethical leadership** is striving for excellence and integrity as one continually develops ethical and moral reasoning while contributing to the common good. Ethical leaders have the courage to live by their principles in all parts of their personal and professional lives.
- **Cultural competence** begins with cultural self-awareness and expands to knowledge of, respect for, and skills to engage with those of other cultures. Culturally competent individuals respect multiple perspectives and are able to successfully negotiate cross-cultural differences.
- **Community engagement** is recognizing needs in the community within which one belongs, then contributing knowledge and working with the community to meet those needs. Community engagement requires extending beyond one's self for the betterment of the community—a process that fosters greater awareness and personal growth. (Missouri State University, 2013).

Missouri State University is the only university in Missouri with a mission in public affairs. (For additional information about Missouri State University and public affairs, visit the website at http://publicaffairs.missouristate.edu/ About.htm.) In addition to Missouri State University's commitment to public affairs, the university has a commitment to service-learning. Service-learning is one vehicle by which Missouri State University carries forward its mission in public affairs and fulfills its designation as a metropolitan university.

Service-learning began on the Missouri State University campus in 1996 through a Faculty Senate resolution and has grown in leaps and bounds over the course of many years. In 1996, the university opened the Office of Citizenship and Service-Learning (CASL; 2013a) on the Missouri State Campus. During the 2012–2013 academic year, 2,725 students contributed 60,973 hours of service to the community; faculty members used this pedagogical tool to underscore academic objectives in 373 service-learning courses. The service-learning hours resulted in a value of $1,158,487.00 worth of contributed hours in service to local, national, and global communities. This represented an 18% increase in service-learning students compared to the 2011–2012 academic year figures of 2,258 students contributing some 60,812 hours to community partners. The mission for the CASL office is to provide academic service-learning opportunities that require effective reflection and have citizenship as a goal—making a difference in communities locally, nationally, and globally.

The CASL office manages and coordinates all academic service-learning programs for the university. The CASL director is responsible for overseeing a number of areas, which include: (a) development of service-learning course curricula; (b) professional development for key stakeholders (students, faculty, staff, administration, community partners); (c) student success and retention in service-learning courses; (d) building community relations; (e) service-learning course enrollment; (f) budget and finance for the department; (g) staff oversight; (h) faculty recruitment; (i) new program development; and (j) assessment.

Institutional Contexts: Missouri State University's eService-Learning Program

In an effort to meet the vision, mission, and goals of the university, coupled with increased student enrollment in online course offerings, the CASL office, along with faculty, staff, and administrators, strives to integrate creative and innovative ways to engage online students in academic course work that uses service-learning as a teaching methodology. Missouri State University's intent is to retain students on its campus, provide cocurricular activities that foster the students' commitment to their community, and prepare these students to become life-long learners. One way Missouri State University works to accomplish this is by requiring freshman students (including those who transfer in with fewer than 24 credit hours), to enroll in the First-Year Experience course during their first semester as an enrolled student.

First-Year Experience, GEP 101 (CASL; 2013b) is a two-credit course and is part of the students' general education requirement. The basic premise of First-Year Experience is to provide a foundation for freshman students to acquaint them with the transition to college life. Topics in this course include time management; financial management; diversity appreciation;

development of reading, research, and critical thinking skills; keys to staying healthy, getting involved on campus, preparing for tests and exams; and note taking. The course also introduces students to the university's public affairs mission of ethical leadership, cultural competence, and community engagement.

According to a recent study (Allen & Seaman, 2013) conducted by the Babson Survey Research Group in conjunction with Pearson and the Sloan Consortium, the number of students enrolled in at least one online course rose by 570,000 and now totals some 6.7 million individuals representing 32% of students enrolled in higher education courses. With this increasing demand for online courses, First-Year Experience was offered for the first time in the online environment in the fall of 2011 with integrated service-learning embedded in the course content. The purpose of integrating eService-Learning into the course was to ensure that important learning outcomes related to civic engagement and public affairs were met, not only through classroom assignments, but through the service-learning experience. Missouri State University determined that students would complete their academic course work in the online environment and the students' service-learning experience would be on-site in a location close to where the student lived, worked, or attended school. In 2012, Waldner, McGorry, & Widener, identified four "emerging types of eService-Learning" (p. 134; see Figure 5.1); Missouri State University uses Waldner, McGorry, and Widener's (2012) Hybrid I model to incorporate into the online First-Year Experience course.

Figure 5.1 Four Emerging Types of eService-Learning

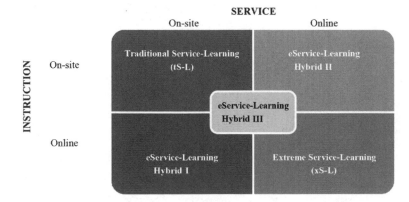

Note. Modified from Waldner, McGorry, and Widener (2012).

Definition: *Hybrid I*—Instruction Online; Service-Learning On-site

Waldner, McGorry, and Widener (2012), as noted in chapter 2 of this book, identify the Hybrid I model when the instruction for the course is provided in an online learning environment but the service-learning takes place on-site. Depending on the number of students enrolled in the course, the geographic locations of those students, and the university's community partner base, this model can present a challenge for faculty in ensuring that all students have a community partner who can provide an experiential service-learning opportunity for the students.

The Missouri State University eService-Learning Model

While service-learning course work at Missouri State University has grown tremendously since 1996, eService-Learning is in its infant stage. Missouri State University offers two types of service-learning options: (a) integrated service-learning (embedded in the course and all students enrolled in the course complete a 15-hour service-learning experience) and (b) designate/component service-learning (students can enroll in a one-credit, 40 hour service-learning experience linked to a designate three-credit course); it is at the discretion of the course instructor and the department as to which type is most appropriate for the course offering. Additionally, the students' service-learning experience can be direct (face-to-face) or indirect; generally determined based on the goals and expected outcomes of the course, the needs of the designated community partner, and the needs of the students coupled with the students' geographic locations. This is an important consideration for faculty in their course design when moving from a traditional service-learning model to the eService-Learning model.

Integrated service-learning for the First-Year Experience course has been a part of the course curriculum for several sections since the fall of 2010; however, as previously noted, the first online First-Year Experience course with embedded service-learning was offered in the fall of 2011. Utilizing the Hybrid I model with integrated service-learning allowed all students enrolled in the course to participate in the service-learning experience. It was determined that one course section, based on enrollment numbers, would be designated as an online First-Year Experience Integrated Service-Learning course whereby students would complete their academic course work (assignments, discussion boards, group projects) online and complete their service-learning experience with a community partner located in the geographic area where the students reside.

Implementing eService-Learning at Missouri State University

The eService-Learning course was developed so that students would have the opportunity to complete their 15 hours of service-learning on-site at a geographic location close to where the students resided or worked. This methodology was selected because geographic data demonstrated that over 50% of the students enrolled resided in locations more than 50 miles from the university campus and surrounding area, and that many of the enrolled students were nontraditional students working to complete their degrees (Enrollment Management and Services, 2014). Nontraditional students are typically over the age of 25; many of the Missouri State University non-traditional students work full-time jobs, have families, or are single-parents. The National Center for Education Statistics (as cited in Pelletier, 2010) "defines nontraditional students as meeting one of seven characteristics" (p. 2); these characteristics include the following: (a) delayed enrollment in an institution of higher education; (b) part-time enrollment; (c) full-time employment; (d) not dependent on a parent's financial resources; (e) has dependents (not including a spouse); (f) is a single parent; and/or (g) does not have a diploma from high school. In fact, in 2008, "just over 1 million of the students enrolled at AASCU [American Association of State Colleges and Universities] institutions were 25 or older" (p. 2).

While Missouri State University values the many service-learning courses offered on its campus and the important contributions the student population makes in the Springfield, Missouri, community and beyond, Missouri State University also understands the many challenges that nontraditional students face when attempting to complete service-learning; challenges such as time constraints, family responsibilities, and geographic divides. These challenges often prevent the nontraditional population of students from completing service-learning in a traditional manner. Thus, great care is taken to ensure that online students receive the same experiential service-learning opportunities that traditional service-learning students receive through utilizing the Hybrid I model.

The First-Year Experience with integrated service-learning or integrated eService-Learning course syllabus was developed utilizing the goals and objectives for the First-Year Experience course coupled with the university's general education requirements and integrated service-learning requirements. The course syllabus included a paragraph that introduced enrolled students to service-learning course requirements and provided detailed instruction as to how service-learning would be achieved in the course. The course syllabus was reviewed and approved by the CASL Oversight Committee (a committee designated by the Faculty Senate) to ensure that the course content was academically rigorous and the required service-learning elements were in place. Course syllabi, for any service-learning course, must be reviewed and approved by the CASL Oversight Committee prior to course implementation.

As a part of the Missouri State University eService-Learning course syllabi, students are provided with examples of how they might complete their eService-Learning experience within the communities where they work or reside. Students, with the assistance of the course instructor and the CASL office, determine where the students complete their eService-Learning experience and how (direct or indirect) their service would be conducted. Students then prepare a proposal outlining what their experience would look like. The following is an example of the eService-Learning requirement that is to be placed in the course syllabus.

Service-Learning Course Requirement For All Service-Learning Courses Including eService-Learning

This service-learning section of GEP 101 is designed to maximize your success at Missouri State. Success at Missouri State includes much more than your academic achievements (GPA, writing skills, critical thinking skills). Success includes commitment to values, increased self-efficacy (or the belief that you can attain certain goals), leadership, interpersonal skills, and engagement in the campus and community.

Integrated Service-Learning (ISL) that incorporates a community service experience with classroom instruction has been integrated into this course to provide a community based learning experience. Service-Learning addresses the practice of citizenship and promotes an awareness of and participation in public affairs. The Integrated Service-Learning Course requires a minimum of 15 hours of unpaid service with a not-for-profit community organization, government agency or public service provider. Potential community partners include: (Rare Breed, Christian Health Care, Boys and Girls Club, CASA, Greene County Health Department, Robberson Community School, USDA, LA Human Rights Commission Bullying Project, etc.)

The community service placement will relate to the course learning objectives as outlined in this syllabus. Reflection assignments are assigned to help students understand discipline concepts and develop higher order critical thinking skills. Additionally, this course provides students with real world experience that can be included on resumes, offers the ability to test career choices, to apply theories and concepts learned in class and make connections to the real world, and the opportunity to have a positive impact in our community. To assess the integration of the service-learning portion of this course, CASL staff will administer an online assessment during the last three weeks of the semester. The evaluation results will assist your instructor in the further development of this course, especially as it relates to the service-learning project. Results are provided to your instructor after the final grades are submitted to the Registrar's Office.

The 15-hour unpaid integrated service-learning experience is an integral part of the course. This section was designed based upon research that shows service-learning's significant positive effects on important outcomes measures such as those listed above: academic performance, values, self-efficacy, leadership, and engagement. As you interact with your classmates and the community, you'll have a chance to solve problems and communicate effectively, deal with others who are unlike you, develop greater self-understanding, and positively impact your community. (CASL, 2012)

Because service-learning links academic learning to the community and provides students with opportunities to develop the skills, sensitivities, and commitments necessary for effective citizenship in a democracy, and because the First-Year Experience course content covers many themes, the Missouri State University public affairs mission is used as the academic framework for the students' service-learning experience. This allows students to engage in a variety of service-learning opportunities that encourages critical thinking and focus on community-based problem solving or in addressing social justice issues; the students then reflect on their service-learning experience, linking it back to the public affairs mission course content. It is at the discretion of the instructor, in conjunction with the CASL office, to provide service-learning options for students. Students have the opportunity to select one or more options to complete a minimum of 15 hours of service and then reflect on their experience.

During the fall 2013 semester, eService-Learning students enrolled in the First-Year Experience online course were provided with additional eService-Learning opportunities (see Table 5.1). These opportunities were developed through collaborative efforts between the CASL office, the course instructor, and the public affairs office at Missouri State University, and provided options for those online students who lived close to campus and tied specifically to the university's annual public affairs theme and the university's Common Reader program for first-year students.

Technology Utilized With eService-Learning Courses

Missouri State University utilizes Blackboard as the learning management system (LMS) for all course work, including online learning courses. eService-Learning students use Blackboard, which is password protected, to submit their service-learning proposals for approval. Students also post their proposal on an online discussion board to receive input, feedback, and comments from their classmates.

TABLE 5.1

Examples of eService-Learning Experiences for Missouri State University Students Enrolled in the Online First-Year Experience Course

Option	Social Justice Issue	Community-Based Need	Community Partner
1	Youth homelessness	Provide activities for homeless youth and teens	Rare Breed in Springfield, Missouri, or a homeless shelter in your community
2	Poverty, scarce resources	Provide housing for those with limited financial resources	Habitat for Humanity build
3	Drugs and crime	Provide after-school opportunities for children in low-income areas	Robberson Community School program in Springfield, Missouri, or an elementary or middle school in the community where you reside
4	Disaster relief	Rebuild Joplin (Fall break project ONLY)	Catholic Charities of Southern Missouri
5	Reading literacy	Provide after-school reading opportunities for children who struggle with reading	Boys and Girls Club (various locations throughout Missouri and in other states)
6	Bullying	Programs to prevent bullying in schools	LA Human Rights Commission; indirect service-learning opportunity for program development, research, etc.
7	Scarce resources	Develop education programs for middle school and high school students to promote appropriate use of resources within our communities	USDA; community schools; Boys and Girls Clubs, etc.
8	Hunger in developing countries	Box food to be shipped to developing countries (November activity)	Friends Against Hunger, Springfield, Missouri; Food Bank programs in your local community
9	Preserving history and heritage	Oral history project	Various long-term care facilities, nursing homes, assisted living facilities

Tying It All Together: Creating Course Reflection Opportunities for eService-Learning Students

Service-learning requires students, whether in the seated or online class environment, to complete reflection exercises demonstrating that they understand how their classroom course content links to their service-learning experience in a way that is impactful and benefits their community partner, as well as themselves. This section discusses three options: the first option has been traditionally utilized for service-learning students; the two additional options have been recently implemented during the fall 2013 semester, as alternative methods for course reflection.

Option 1

Students complete reflection exercises using a reflection journal. In addition to fostering writing skills, using a reflection journal engages students in thinking critically about their experience and connecting the experience to their course work. The First-Year Experience eService-Learning course option 1 combines reflection writing with the creation of a PowerPoint presentation to showcase the students' service-learning experience, how their experience relates to the university's public affairs mission, and how their experience made a difference in their community. Upon completion of the students' service-learning hours, students prepare a three- to five-page reflection paper. Students are asked to think critically about the experience they have gained and identify and describe how community engagement inspired them to become better students and citizens. Students must connect what they have learned in the course about ethical leadership, cultural competence, community engagement (the three public affairs pillars) to their service-learning experience. Students are also encouraged to include pictures and graphics in their written reflection. The reflection activities are what tie together the eService-Learning experience with the students' academic course content.

Option 2

Students create a PowerPoint presentation based on their eService-Learning experience. The PowerPoint presentation must incorporate one of the three public affairs pillars of ethical leadership, cultural competence, or community engagement, and must include information from at least two sources (the first source might be information about the community partner and the second source might be information about the community-based problem or social justice issue that was addressed during the service-learning experience). In order for the PowerPoint presentation to be effective, it must have at least 15 slides. Any sources must be cited in the PowerPoint presentation.

Option 3

Students create a YouTube video providing information about the eService-Learning experience and the community-based problem or social justice issue addressed. The video should be no less than 3 minutes in length and no more than 5 minutes in length, incorporate one of the three public affairs pillars (ethical leadership, cultural competence, or community engagement), and include two scholarly sources. Sources must be cited in the video.

Missouri State University Data Collection of eService-Learning

Missouri State University and the CASL office acknowledge the importance of assessments and understand the impact of data and evaluations on the development of strategic plans, goals, and key performance indicators. These data are important when working to gain accreditation through various bodies including, but not limited to, the Higher Learning Commission, the Carnegie Classification designation, and the President's Honor Roll designation, as well as with the many academic-specific accreditors. Data collected are vital to and drive decisions the university makes regarding enrollment, funding, ongoing program development, expansion of course sections, allocation of resources, and building community relations.

Fall 2013 With Optional eService-Learning

For the fall 2013 semester, and because of the nature of the course (service-learning was optional), a mini-pilot study was conducted and a post-course survey was administered (see "Service-Learning Course Requirement" on p. 75 of this chapter) to those who selected service-learning as part of their course; students who did not select the service-learning option were not surveyed. The data captured in the survey relate to the university's public affairs mission, which identifies the students' commitment to and their perspectives on the importance of community engagement, cultural competence, and ethical leadership.

Participant Demographics
Of the 27 enrolled students in the course, 16 students (60% of the enrolled students) opted to participate in an eService-Learning experience. Of the 16 eService-Learning participants, 12 participants (3 males, and 9 females) completed the survey. Thirty-three percent of the participants identified

as traditional students while 66% of the participants identified themselves as nontraditional students. Fifty-eight percent of the eService-Learning students identified that they were full-time students; 42% of the students identified themselves as part-time students. Of the eService-Learning survey participant students, 66% identified that they were employed full-time, 17% identified that they were employed part-time, and 17% identified that they were not employed (CASL, 2013b).

Post-Course Survey Questions
To measure students' commitment to ethical leadership, cultural competence, and community engagement—the three pillars of Missouri State University's public affairs mission—students were asked to respond to statements associated with each public affairs pillar using a 7-point Likert scale (1 = *strongly disagree*, 7 = *strongly agree*). This Public Affairs Scale survey was developed and validated by Jef Cornelius-White and Chantal Levesque (2009), provost fellows at Missouri State University, as a part of their research. The survey questions are identified in Table 5.2.

   Data for the mini-pilot study were collected at the end of the semester for students who opted to complete service-learning as part of their GEP 101 First-year Experience course, and the results of the data will serve as a baseline by which the Missouri State University CASL office will measure future GEP 101 First-Year Experience courses with integrated eService-Learning.

TABLE 5.2
Public Affairs Scale Results for Fall 2013 GEP 101 Online eService-Learning Course

Community Engagement (CE): N = 12			
Question #	*Statement*	*Mean Score*	*Standard Deviation*
CE1	Volunteering will help me succeed in my own profession.	5.75	1.14
CE2	I plan to do some volunteer work next year.	5.67	1.30
CE3	Volunteering makes me feel like I am contributing to the community.	6.42	0.90
CE4	I do things for a cause bigger than myself.	6.25	0.97
CE5	I feel an obligation to contribute to the community.	6.17	0.94

(Continues)

TABLE 5.2   (*Continued*)

Cultural Competence (CC): N = 12

Question #	Statement	Mean Score	Standard Deviation
CC1	I am able to communicate effectively with people from different cultures.	5.83	1.03
CC2	I understand the challenges faced by people from different cultures.	5.50	1.09
CC3	I have been involved in organizations providing services to people from different cultural backgrounds.	5.17	1.53
CC4	In the future, I will travel to other countries to better understand culture and diversity.	4.83	1.70
CC5	I can easily relate to people that are different from me.	5.83	1.19

Ethical Leadership (EL): N = 12

Question #	Statement	Mean Score	Standard Deviation
EL1	When I am in groups, I am thoughtful of other people's feelings.	6.25	0.97
EL2	I am dependable and reliable.	6.50	0.80
EL3	I try to make certain that my actions never intentionally harm another person.	6.58	0.67
EL4	I am aware of what kind of person I am.	6.33	0.79
EL5	When working in groups, I try to assure everyone's voice is heard before a decision is reached.	6.50	0.80

Note. Office of Citizenship and Service-Learning (CASL, 2013b).

Moving the Needle Forward: New Assessment Efforts

Since assessment data are vital to moving all service-learning programs forward, the CASL office will implement a new assessment process beginning with the fall 2014 service-learning courses. This new assessment will be administered through an end-of-semester survey and will include both the Public Affairs Scale (previously used) and the new service-learning course outcomes approved by the CASL Oversight Committee. The new survey will not only be used to measure students' commitment to Missouri State University's public affairs mission using the Public Affairs Scale, but also provide a tool to assess and evaluate service-learning student course outcomes from both the students' and the professor's perspectives; one survey for faculty and one survey for students. The new CASL Service-Learning Assessment Tool was developed using the American Association of Community Colleges assessment tool as the framework. The American Association of Community Colleges assessment tool's framework examines expected outcomes from faculty teaching service-learning course work and students enrolled in service-learning course work. The assessment tool evaluates the following six outcome areas:

1. Critical thinking
2. Communication
3. Career and teamwork
4. Civic responsibility
5. Global understanding and citizenship
6. Academic development and educational success

This new adapted survey uses a 5-point Likert scale (1 = *strongly disagree*, 5 = *strongly agree*) and focuses on desired service-learning student outcomes for all students enrolled in a service-learning course. Data collected during the fall 2014 semester will be evaluated and results will be provided to faculty, students, community partners, Missouri State University's Office of Assessment, and Missouri State University administration during the spring of 2015. The Missouri State University CASL Service-Learning Course Outcomes to be measured can be found in this chapter's appendix. Posttest surveys will continue to be administered at the end of the semester and will measure both the service-learning faculty member's perspective on completed outcomes as a part of the service-learning course and the student's perspective. It should be noted that the new survey instrument will be administered to all faculty and students engaged in service-learning (traditional service-learning or eService-Learning).

General Recommendations for Other Colleges and Universities

When considering eService-Learning for your academic course, the CASL office recommends that colleges and universities consider providing resources and professional development opportunities for faculty who want to utilize service-learning as a teaching methodology, including that of eService-Learning. The Missouri State University CASL office provides a number of professional development opportunities such as monthly workshops, an annual service-learning conference, and one-on-one trainings and assistance with course syllabus design. Additionally, the CASL office provides an extensive service-learning library (housed in the service-learning office), to assist faculty with understanding the importance of and the role educational leadership plays in the success and sustainability of programs, including academic eService-Learning. The CASL office also houses a large database of community partners that includes community partner contact information and needs of the community partners. This allows the CASL staff to assist faculty in selecting community partners that align with course content and students enrolled in the course can meet the community partners' needs; thus providing reciprocal relationships.

Colleges and universities might also consider how service-learning course syllabi are reviewed and approved to ensure the academic rigor of the service-learning course and that required course elements are identified within a service-learning course syllabus. At Missouri State University, the CASL office works with the CASL Oversight Committee to ensure the academic rigor of the service-learning course syllabus, associated service-learning experience, and reflection activity. At Missouri State University the CASL Oversight Committee is comprised of a faculty member from each of the six academic colleges, the chair-elect for Faculty Senate, and the CASL director.

With a focus on learning-centered leadership and student-centered learning, the CASL office also recommends that colleges and universities consider utilizing components of the Vanderbilt Assessment of Leadership in Education, identified in the research of Goldring, Porter, Murphy, Elliott, and Cravens (2009), in their review of service-learning syllabi. Figure 5.2, developed by the CASL office, depicts the core components of high standards for student learning as identified by Goldring et al. (2009) and as utilized at Missouri State University.

Colleges and universities that offer, or that are considering offering, service-learning courses, including eService-Learning, might consider adopting the core components of high standards suggested by Goldring et al. (2009) as a foundation for service-learning course work on their campuses.

Figure 5.2 CASL Core Assessment Components

Note. Developed by K. Nordyke, Citizenship and Service-Learning, Missouri State University. Based on the framework for assessment provided by Goldring, Porter, Murphy, Elliott, and Cravens (2009) in the Vanderbilt Assessment of Leadership in Education.

In addition to providing faculty with opportunities and resources, the CASL office also recommends that colleges and universities provide for transparency of their service-learning programs and data. Beginning in the fall of 2014, the CASL office, in conjunction with Missouri State University's Office of Assessment and Research and the Office of Web and New Media, will begin development on a service-learning dashboard that will be housed on the CASL website. The CASL dashboard will provide key stakeholders with the university's ratings and scores based on results from the Institutional Self-Assessment Tool for Service-Learning (Furco, 2002) or other assessment tools, along with the results from the Missouri State University CASL Service-Learning Student Outcomes Measurement Survey Tool. The CASL dashboard will provide additional data on student success; retention; and drop, fail, withdraw (DFW) rates for service-learning

Figure 5.3 Missouri State University Office of Citizenship and Service-Learning (CASL) Sample Dashboard to Support Key Performance Indicators

Note. Developed by the Missouri State University Office of Citizenship and Service-Learning (CASL; 2014). Currently in development.

courses. Communicating the institution's commitment to service-learning as a vehicle to support the university's public affairs mission, along with sustainability of the service-learning program, the new dashboard will: (a) identify and communicate the impact of service-learning on course outcomes and student success and retention rates relating to service-learning course work; and (b), provide survey and focus group feedback from community partner assessments. This information then provides a lens in which our constituents can view the strengths, successes, and opportunities for improvement at all service-learning levels. A draft sample of the CASL Dashboard is shown in Figure 5.3.

As the development of the dashboard is in its infancy, we encourage readers to check the CASL website (www.missouristate.edu/casl) for progress and results.

Benefits of eService-Learning Hybrid I

As demonstrated throughout this book and within this chapter, there are many ways in which eService-Learning can be modeled; chapter 5 has focused on using Hybrid I model. It is recommended that the Hybrid I model be used when students are enrolled in an online service-learning course and the students reside in areas that prevent them from completing their service-learning experience with community partners close to campus. This model allows students to complete their course work online and complete their service-learning experience face-to-face with a community partner located in the student's geographic area.

The foundation for service-learning is the same for a seated or an online course; however, what differs for eService-Learning is the selection of the hybrid model that best suits your methodology for providing your students with a great experience. It is my hope that this chapter has provided you with ideas that can be utilized for transforming your online course into an eService-Learning course, thus providing your students with a great opportunity to engage in community-based problem solving and address social justice issues through high-impact experiential learning—eService-Learning.

References

Allen, I. E., & Seaman, J. (2013). *Changing course: Ten years of tracking online education in the United States.* Babson Park, MA: Babson Survey Research Group.

Cornelius-White, J., & Levesque, C. (2009). *Construction and validation of the public affairs scale: A report on the Missouri State University public affairs mission.* Springfield, MO: Missouri State University.

Enrollment Management and Services. (2014, November 11). Missouri State University. Retrieved from http://www.missouristate.edu/enrollmentmanagement

Furco, A. (2002). *Self-assessment rubric for the institutionalization of service-learning in higher education.* Retrieved May 2013, from: http://www.nationalservice.gov/sites/default/files/resource/r4179-furco-rubric.pdf

Goldring, E., Porter, A., Murphy, J., Elliott, S. N., & Cravens, X. (2009). Assessing learning-centered leadership: Connections to research, professional standards, and current practices. *Leadership and Policy in Schools, 8,* 1–36. doi:10.1080/15700760802014951

Missouri State University. (n.d.) *Mission statement.* Retrieved from http://www.missouristate.edu/about/missionstatement.htm

Missouri State University. (2010). About the university. Retrieved from http://www.missouristate.edu/about/

Missouri State University. (2013). *What is public affairs.* Retrieved from: http://publicaffairs.missouristate.edu/About.htm

Office of Citizenship and Service-Learning (CASL). (2012). *Oversight committee handbook.* Office of Citizenship and Service-Learning, p. 1–70.

Office of Citizenship and Service-Learning (CASL). (2013a). Missouri State University. Retrieved from http://missouristate.edu/casl

Office of Citizenship and Service-Learning (CASL). (2013b). *Public affairs scale Results fall 2013 GEP 101 online eservice-learning course.* Missouri State University. Retrieved from MSU Survey Monkey database.

Pelletier, S. G. (2010). Success for adult students. *Public Purpose,* 2–6.

Prentice, M., & Robinson, G. (2010). *Improving student learning outcomes with service learning.* American Association of Community Colleges in conjunction with Learn & Serve Higher Education. Retrieved from http://www.aacc.nche.edu/Resources/aaccprograms/horizons/Documents/slorb_jan2010.pdf

Waldner, L. S., McGorry, S. Y., & Widener, M. C. (2012). E-service-learning: The evolution of service-learning to engage a growing online student population. *Journal of Higher Education Outreach and Engagement,* 16(2), 123–150.

APPENDIX
Missouri State University CASL Service-Learning Outcomes

Critical Thinking

By the end of the course, students will know how to do the following:

1. Identify problems/social-justice issues in the community
2. Understand the root cause of the problem/issue identified
3. Generate alternative solutions to address the problem/issue

Communication

By the end of the course, students will be able to do the following:

1. Demonstrate the effective use of oral, written and listening communication skills

Career and Teamwork

By the end of the course, students will be able to do the following:

1. Demonstrate strong leadership skills
2. Be able to work well in teams and with others
3. Obtain the skills to work in a career that will make contributions to society
4. Recognize that what they do in their jobs or work might have implications beyond the local community

Civic Responsibility

By the end of the course, students will be able to do the following:

1. Understand the importance of contributing to their community
2. Be concerned about local community issues and problems
3. Identify ways in which they could improve their neighborhoods in the future
4. Believe they can have a positive impact on local social problems

Academic Development and Educational Success

By the end of the course, students will be able to do the following:

1. Learn better when courses include service-learning experiences
2. Understand the connection between their academic learning at this university and real-life experiences
3. Be committed to finishing their educational goals (either completing a degree or taking all of the classes that they had planned on taking when they first enrolled at this university)

Public Affairs Mission:

By the end of the course, students will be able to do the following:

1. Recognize the importance of contributing their knowledge and experiences to their own community and the broader society
2. Recognize the importance of scientific principles in the generation of sound public policy
3. Recognize and respect multiple perspectives and cultures
4. Articulate their value systems, act ethically within the context of a democratic society, and demonstrate engaged and principled leadership

Adapted with permission from Prentice, M., & Robinson, G. (2010). *Improving student learning outcomes with service learning.* American Association of Community Colleges. Retrieved from www.aacc.nche.edu/Resources/aaccprograms/horizons/Documents/slorb_jan2010.pdf

The Service-Learning Student and Faculty Survey Instrument to assess the Service-Learning Student Outcomes incorporates the Missouri State University Public Affairs Scale developed by Jef Cornelius-White and Chantal Levesque (2009).

The suggested service-learning course outcomes as shown in this appendix can be applied to both Traditional Service-Learning and eService-Learning courses.

6

HYBRID II

A Model Design for Web Development

Pauline Mosley

A hybrid eService-Learning web design course that meets the objectives of the class and that uses the community as a research laboratory is a powerful pedagogical strategy. This approach also promotes effective student learning. Web development is a challenging area that is of increasing interest to students in information systems and other disciplines. Those who teach introductory web design courses know how difficult it is to simulate a real-world setting for course projects. One major objective of these courses focuses on web usability and all of the other human factors that relate to the user experience on the web. It is a challenge to design projects that meet these objectives. It is necessary to complement classroom lectures with hands-on laboratory exercises to reinforce the material, but providing meaningful laboratory exercises is problematic. The benefits of service-learning are evident, and this experience is worthwhile for our students. However, we often must justify why it needs to be integrated into web design courses.

This chapter shares with the reader a qualitative research study implementing the Hybrid II eService-Learning model. This study was conducted over 5 years with Pace University students and with local Westchester, New York, nonprofit organizations. This chapter demonstrates how students experience the political, social, and ethical problems and the competitiveness that exist in the workplace by working with real users. Last, this chapter reveals how the civic component of this model transcends the course to establish connections between academics and society.

Service-Learning at Pace University

Pace University interprets its mission of *opportunitas* as a mandate to collaborate across constituencies, both internal and external, to create an "engaged campus." Hence, it has as the hallmark of its core curriculum a civic engagement and public values component. This component requires all students to complete a three-credit service-learning course before graduation. The course requires students to participate in an organized service activity that requires 10 to 20 hours of service. When students reflect on their service activity, they increase their understanding and application of the course content and enhance their sense of civic responsibility.

Students can select from 29 service-learning course offerings in various curriculum areas; however, interestingly, many choose to take a technology-based service-learning course to fulfill this core requirement. Over 87% of the students enrolled in technology-based service-learning courses are non-technology majors. This course, though technology based, still must fulfill the core course learning goals and objectives.

What Is a Hybrid II eService-Learning Model?

The structure of a service-learning course lends itself to myriad flexible models of civic engagement (see Table 6.1 for a description of several models). Regardless of the model, the instructor usually has a large-scale project that requires students to complete a minimum of 15 to 20 hours of community service and to submit a reflective journal at the end of the semester. This actively engaging civic experience goes beyond the textbook, classroom, and subject matter and raises the level of digital inclusion.

The eService-Learning Hybrid II model noted in Figure 6.1 encompasses all four models. In this model, the course is taught off-line but the students and community partners must work together online. The course meets for 2 hours a week, with 1 hour online, and attracts about 25 students at each offering. The course has been among the most popular elective courses in the Computer Information Systems Department. The prerequisite for the course is CIS 101: Introduction to Computers. No math or computer science prerequisite courses are required. As part of the requirements, the course

TABLE 6.1
Models of Service-Learning

Model	*Goal*
Civic-based	The learning goal for the civic-based service-learning model is to promote civic engagement.
Problem-based	The learning goal for the problem-based service-learning model is to solve real, community-based problems.
Consulting-based	The learning goal for the consulting-based service-learning model is to apply technical expertise to community needs.
Community-based action research	The learning goal for the community-based action research service-learning model is to apply action research methodologies to a perceived community-based problem.

Figure 6.1 Hybrid II eService-Learning Model

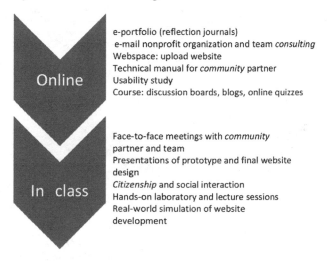

Online

e-portfolio (reflection journals)
e-mail nonprofit organization and team *consulting*
Webspace: upload website
Technical manual for *community* partner
Usability study
Course: discussion boards, blogs, online quizzes

In class

Face-to-face meetings with *community* partner and team
Presentations of prototype and final website design
Citizenship and social interaction
Hands-on laboratory and lecture sessions
Real-world simulation of website development

has two exams (a midterm and a final), five lab assignments, and a mandatory semester-long service-learning project. The project carries about 20% to 25% of the semester grade. The course has a lab component and a lecture component. In the labs, students can have hands-on experience with HTML and web authoring tools such as Dreamweaver and Photoshop. During the lab hours, students work on different problems individually or in groups. These labs are designed to help students better understand the concepts and functionality of designing a website.

Course Development

Students are presented with a nonprofit organization desirous of a website or a nonprofit organization with a poorly designed website, and they are instructed to implement a solution. This eService-Learning aspect of the course presents them with real-world problems, and it uses a blend of off-line education coupled with online pedagogy. This experience goes beyond the textbook, classroom, and subject matter. Integrating the eService-Learning Hybrid II model into a web design curriculum produces web designers. This model also educates students about their responsibility to effectively empower their communities with blended technology.

Table 6.2 shows a sample list of subjects covered in the web design course per week. One can clearly see how an instructor can typically assign 8 to 10 weekly projects per semester. In this approach, the students often fail to see how each topic is interrelated. Each topic is treated as a separate unit, and knowing what to use when and for what reason is lost. With this approach, it is very difficult to reinforce concepts from weeks 1 through 4 in weeks 6 through 14 because the labs are strictly focusing on the specific topic.

In Table 6.3, the course was modified to include a large eService-Learning project, assigned concurrently with the topics for web design and development. The goal is for students to begin thinking about solutions for this project at the same time that they receive lectures on web design features, concepts, and usage. This approach forces the students to think critically and to work as a team both online and off-line. The students know that at the end of the semester, they must have developed a functional website. Because the client may want additional hyperlinks or tables added (as an example), all topics are constantly being reinforced. Thus, to successfully complete the website, the students need to know the topics from week 1 through week 13.

What Is Done Online?

For technology-mediated learning environments to be pedagogically effective, faculty need to incorporate interactive features such as online discussions, assessment, and feedback that directly contribute to student learning (Hazari & Schnorr, 1999). This course used the Blackboard 7.0 Management System (a course management system) to facilitate a technology-mediated learning environment. The online components of this course provided students with experiential learning (Rogers & Freiberg, 1994), and they used features and teaching methodologies that went beyond convenience-based features such as providing the syllabus, schedule, and other course documents. The online components also developed students' communication skills, ability to work well in teams (including virtual teams), and analytical and problem-solving skills.

TABLE 6.2
Web Design Course With Small Projects

Week 1	Week 2	Week 3	Week 4	Week 5	Week 6	Week 7	Week 8	Weeks 9–10	Weeks 11–12	Week 13	Week 14
Intro	Basic HTML	Hyperlinks	Graphics	Tables	Presentation	Forms	Style sheets	Animation	Flash	Usability study	Presentation
	Lab	Lab	Lab	Lab		Lab		Lab	Lab		

TABLE 6.3
Web Design Course With eService-Learning Large-Scale Project

Week 1	Week 2	Week 3	Week 4	Week 5	Week 6	Week 7	Week 8	Weeks 9–10	Weeks 11–12	Week 13	Week 14
Intro	Basic HTML	Hyperlinks	Graphics	Tables	Presentation	Forms	Style sheets	Animation	Flash	Usability study	Presentation

Group project: Create and design a website for a nonprofit organization.

The website development teams used the Blackboard discussion board feature to establish a protocol for communication. Thus, if a team member was absent, he or she could still contribute to the overall development of the project. In addition, the students used the e-portfolio feature of Blackboard to capture their journey from the inception of the website to the final product. Each week, students were asked to provide an update on what they did, how their community partner was responding, and how their teammates were cooperating. These updates were critical online components that reinforced and supported the course off-line.

Interaction and feedback are vital in improving the quality and success of learning with online components (Cornell & Martin, 1997). Consequently, several online questionnaires were integrated into this course, enabling students to comment on class lectures, topics, and other concerns relevant to the instructional process. Students were given several questionnaires throughout the semester to assist the instructor in pacing the lectures and labs. The instructor controlled the flow of learning and evaluated teaching strategies by referring to the students' feedback. Use of online testing, multimedia materials, and an interactive discussion board provided a strong technological dimension to the course that kept the class connected even after class hours. Online components were a good supplement to face-to-face classes. Students considered this component a course strength and stated that it facilitated collaborative efforts for their teaching projects.

What Is Done Off-line?

Pace students self-selected themselves into teams with three or four members. Each team elected a project leader, web designer, and web coordinator. The teams with four members shared dual roles so that each team member had a role. The project leader for each team picked out of a hat the site that his or her team was to redesign, resulting in two teams developing the same site.

During the four weeks of design and information gathering, the Pace students worked with their respective teams in the design, layout, and prototyping of their site. In the fifth week of class, the clients came to the university to meet with the vying teams and to see the prototypes. During the next four weeks, the teams modified the site to incorporate the client's feedback, performed usability testing and analysis of the site, and prepared for their final presentation. In the tenth week of class, termed *presentation week*, the clients returned to view the final products and to receive the sites on CD, along with a technical manual. The clients were then given a week to "play" with each team's site, after which the clients had to choose which team met the requirements best.

Synergy of Civic Engagement and Course Content

In general, technology instructors tend to build the students' basic skills for a significant portion of their courses. The acquisition of these basic skills helps to build a cumulative aptitude in the students. Technology-based courses, however, also need to develop theoretical understanding of the technology and the use of higher level composite skills. Developing critical analysis, technical fluency, and intellectual breadth are a few of the learning goals for the IS/IT curriculum (shown in Figure 6.1).

For web design and development instructors, aligning the IT content course goals and service-learning objectives can be challenging. Some instructors attempt to cover as many objectives as possible and treat each course objective as an independent "black box."

Students may fail to see the correlation between courses taken in fulfillment of the university core requirement and the IT content course. The service-learning web project remedies this problem. All semester long, the instructor has the opportunity to show correlation between what students have already taken and are taking and what they are currently learning with the project. The project requires them to use presentation skills. A speech class taken a semester ago is very handy when students are presenting their website to the community partner. Project management, teamwork, troubleshooting, and many other skills sets can be reinforced with the service-learning project.

Figure 6.1 Continuum of Service-Learning Project Goals

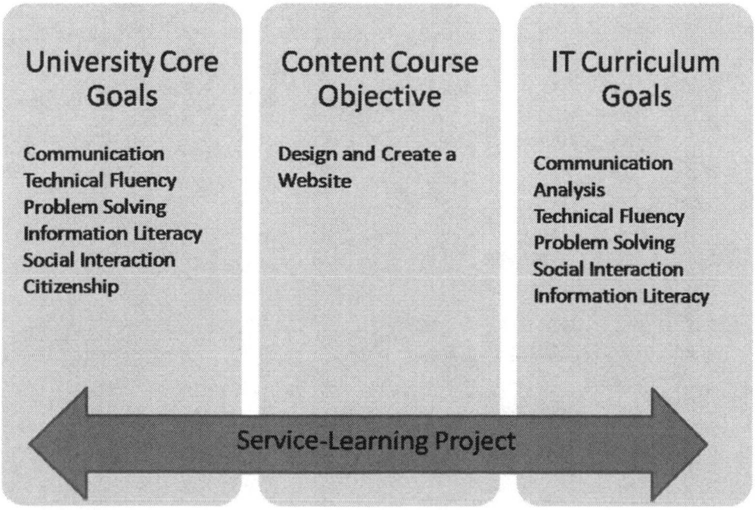

Major goals of most IS/IT courses are to introduce new technological techniques and methods as strategic tools for solving technological problems and encourage students to think independently of the technology. Too often students rely on the technology to solve problems for them rather than determine if the technology is being used correctly. Many IS/IT courses that involve learning a technological tool require students to gain hands-on knowledge of the technology for the duration of the semester. The instructor may require students to complete weekly exercises to demonstrate proficiency and comprehension of the technology.

Although this approach serves a purpose, it does not provide the students with an understanding of the usefulness of advanced technology or allow the students to conceptualize solutions to problems that are not so well defined. In addition, students should get an introduction to the collaboration necessary in large-group IT environments. Immersion in such an environment greatly benefits their appreciation for technological fluency, problem solving, and communication skills.

eService-Learning is a mechanism by which students will apply theories they learn in the classroom to a real-life need within the community. This learning is the thread that weaves these objectives together. Because the eService-Learning component is project-based, the civic engagement experience encourages students to use everything that they have learned in the course. The course includes a period of reflection at the culmination of students' eService-Learning experiences. Students can see if they recognize how knowledge units relate to one another within the course and with other courses.

The inclusion of eService-Learning into the curriculum often demands a reconfiguration of traditional methods of learning and teaching. As with any new approach, the instructor has to make changes, and integrating eService-Learning into a course is no different. This transformation in pedagogy poses new challenges for instructors and students. Changing the focus of the traditional technology-based course from individual lab assignments to the use of large-scale projects reinforces the knowledge units from the university core and from the IS/IT curriculum.

Nonprofit Organizations: The eService-Learning Partners

This research employed a quasi-experimental research design. The participants for the study were 43 Westchester nonprofit organizations, as shown in Table 6.4. Data for this study were gathered as part of a larger study during the years 2008–2012. Participants for this study were recruited based on the researcher's prior profession as a corporate technology trainer for major

TABLE 6.4
**Community Partner Profile for Respondents of
Questionnaires and Interviews**

Agency Type	Nonprofit Organization	Website (if available)	Sample Size
Animal shelters	Shelter Pet Alliance	shelterpetalliance.org	n = 2
	Yonkers Animal Shelter		
Arts	Croton Cortlandt Arts Center	cccarts.org	n = 4
	Hudson Theatre Group	hudsonstage.com	
	Summit Music Festival	summitmusicfestival.org	
	Westchester Concert Singers	westchesterconcertsingers.org	
Churches	Downtown Music at Grace Church		n = 1
Day care centers	Lois Bronz Children's Center		n = 4
	Progressive Steps For Life		
	Ossining Children's Center	ossiningchildrenscenter.org	
	Harrison Children's Center		
Education	Greenburgh Central 7 Arts Program	greenburg.k12.ny.us/arts/welcome.htm	n = 9
	Greenburgh Technology Department		
	Highview Elementary School		
	Opportunity Center		
	Pace Welcome Center		
	R.J. Bailey School		
	Teacher Center for Westchester	ewteachercenter.org	
	Woodlands Math Department		
	San Andres Educational Program		
Health	Cancer Support Team	cancersupportteam.org	n = 3
	Open Book		
	The Loft		

(*Continues*)

TABLE 6.4   *(Continued)*

Agency Type	Nonprofit Organization	Website (if available)	Sample Size
Libraries	The Warner Library	Warnerlibrary.org	*n* = 1
Nursing homes	Glen Island Nursing Home	Glenislandcarecenter.com/home.htm	*n* = 3
	United Hebrew Geriatric Center	unitedhebrewgeriatric.org/volunteer_memoirs.asp	
	Westchester Center for Rehab & Nursing		
Social services	Child Abuse Prevention Center	preventchildabuse.net	*n* = 4
	Family Service Society of Yonkers		
	Human Development Serv. of West.	hdsw.org	
	The Hartsdale Fire Department	hartsdalefire.com/index.html	
Special interests groups	National Council of Negro Women		*n* = 4
	Human Development Center		
	Historical Society		
	Martin Luther King Commission		
Shelters	Caring for the Homeless of Peekskill		*n* = 2
	SHORE		
Youth services	Jewish Council of Yonkers	jewishcouncil.info	*n* = 5
	Rye Youth Council		
	Tomorrow Leaders, Inc.	tomorrowleaders.org	
	YMCA in Yonkers	yoymca.org	
	Hope House		
Total			*N* = 42

Fortune 500 firms. The goal was to obtain a representative cross-section of nonprofit organizations with varying levels of experience and expertise from which meaningful data for the study could be derived.

Participants spanned all functional areas and were diverse in their missions. The participants included 12 varying agencies. Thus, the data collected from these participants can be considered a good representation of the domain of possible responses. At the end of each semester, all nonprofit organizations were interviewed for 15 minutes, and they were given a survey to complete. The purpose of the interview was to gain an emic view of how the service-learning partner perceived the overall web design process. Thus, although the planned set of questions served as a guide for the interview, each one proceeded in a slightly different fashion from the other interviews.

The approach used to analyze the data collected from the interviews and the surveys is known among methodologists in the social sciences as *iterative content analysis* and *open coding*. The content analysis revealed a number of common themes in the interview and questionnaire data. The most prevalent emergent theme was the community partner's 92% response rate that Pace University students were an asset to their organization. Table 6.5 summarizes the relative frequency of the responses by the participants.

The Students

Affective learning was assigned to one of two categories: self-knowledge ($n = 200$) or personal growth ($n = 142$). Most entries showing self-knowledge were found in summaries on the overall course experience and in entries after the students presented their web prototype designs to their respective community partners. All of the students were required to respond to the inquiry of how their eService-Learning activity improved their self-knowledge or personal growth. This result is revealed in Table 6.6, where service-learning for both personal growth and self-knowledge ($n = 70$) is shown; two students failed to complete this assignment.

Personal growth, another form of affective learning, appeared in 142 entries. A vast majority of entries showing personal growth were entries from the overall experience and from how students' perceptions changed after they entered the classroom. This result may be an artifact of the summary assignment that asked students to summarize and reflect on their personal learning. Examples from the overall experience entries include the following:

> This experience was wonderful! I enjoyed working with my community partner and will seriously think about doing web development on the side.

TABLE 6.5
Frequency of the Predominant Themes From Respondents Who Report Sharing This Experience, Inclination, or Belief

Themes Identified in the Responses	*Responses (%)*
Community partner	
Pace University students were an asset to our organization	92
Pace University students understood our organization's mission	87
Pace University students were professional and on time with client	84
The client is satisfied with the final website design	94
Service-learning challenges	
Students were unable to travel to the community partner's site	21
Community partner was unable to articulate what its web presence should be	17
Website challenges	13
Not enough time to complete the website	86
Unable to launch the website successfully	28
Skill sets of the students were inadequate for the level of online presence desired	

I loved working with HTML and being a consultant to my community partner. I hope that they hire me to continue making changes to their site.

At first I didn't like the idea of working in a team, but once we started working on the website, I realized that my work was independent of the teams. I'm also glad to help a community organization obtain an online presence.

Journal entries also demonstrated connective learning and that the Pace students felt personally connected with one another. This result is consistent with research that shows that service-learning brings team members closer to one another (Crabtree, 1998) and that it can change the meaning of being a group member (Godfrey, 1999). In addition, several of the journal entries revealed that students bonded with their community partners. Table 6.6 shows that most of the Pace students interacted socially with their classmates ($n = 77$) and that 55 of them interacted with their service-learning partners.

The impact of eService-Learning on student learning often is traced over a semester or with cross-sectional data. To examine how eService-Learning and web design affect learning over time, we contacted students who took the class 4 years ago (2011). The survey included open-ended questions.

TABLE 6.6
Affective and Connective Learning From eService-Learning and Web Development

Affective Learning Category	Number of Entries	Service-Learning Activities	Social Interactions With Pace Students	Social Interactions With Service-Learning Partner	Mean	SD	Variance
Personal development							
Self-knowledge/personal understanding	200	70	35	25	43.3	23.62	558.3
Personal growth/values development	142	70	42	30	47.3	20.52	421.33
Total	342	140	77	55			
Connective learning							
Connections with the Pace students	88	30	41	17	29.33	12.01	144.33
Connections with the not-for-profit organization	54	19	21	14	18	3.6	13
Connections beyond the course	37	15	12	10	12.33	2.5	6.3
Total	179	64	74	41			

Respondents used a Likert-type scale (1–5) to rate the service-learning activities and web design activities according to how each contributed to content, affective, and connective learning.

The set of questions, reported in Table 6.7, from this survey asked respondents to rate learning from service activity and service-learning activities. Content learning regarding web design was the strongest. A few students strongly agreed that critical thinking or problem-solving skills were stimulated by web design or the service-learning project.

Connective learning also endured. Table 6.7 shows that 5 students strongly agreed that the service-learning activity and 1 strongly agreed that the web design project increased their "sense of connection to a wider world community."

Last, 11 of the respondents reported that the web design project improved their overall knowledge of web design, and 7 responded that it improved their critical thinking skills. The results in Table 6.7 reveal that knowledge acquisition is retained even after the students leave the classroom and complete their service-learning experience. The lingering effects of teamwork and peer-to-peer mentoring still shape how students view learning.

Critical Success Factors for the eService-Learning Hybrid II Model

Three major factors determine the success or failure of a course like this. The first critical success factor is students' technology skill sets. Students' skills in an application-oriented course can be highly varied. The instructor must be cognizant of the potential variance in skills the students bring to the course. The students' skill sets determine how the instructor will present the material and determine how much time to spend on each topic, content details, and overall expectations. Creating student teams with equal skill sets is challenging. However, if students are assessed at the beginning of the course, then establishing well-balanced teams is more likely.

The second critical success factor is the development and design of the eService-Learning Hybrid II model. Having an effective timeline that explores the breadth of each topic at the expense of the depth of coverage requires planning. Determining what topics to teach face-to-face and what topics to teach online is key to the overall success of the course. It is very important to coordinate how the service-learning project will be completed while the students are acquiring the necessary skills needed to complete the project.

The final critical success factor is the dynamics of the community partner. Identifying a nonprofit organization that needs a website and that can

TABLE 6.7
Longer Term Learning Outcomes (N = 12)

How strongly would you agree that service-learning activities:	Mean	SD	How strongly would you agree the web design activities:	Mean	SD
Content knowledge			Content knowledge		
Improved my knowledge of problem-solving skills (SA = 5; A = 4; N = 3)	4.1	0.83	Improved my knowledge of problem-solving skills (SA = 6; S = 4; N = 2)	4.3	0.78
Improved my knowledge of web design (SA = 7; A = 4; N = 1)	4.5	0.67	Improved my knowledge of web design (SA = 11; A = 1)	4.9	0.29
Improved my presentation skills (SA = 4; A = 5; D = 3)	3.8	1.19	Improved my critical thinking skills (SA = 7; A = 4; N = 1)	4.5	0.67
Affective knowledge			Affective knowledge		
Improved my knowledge of myself and what is important to me (SA = 3; A = 3; N = 4; D = 2)	3.5	1.08	Improved my knowledge of myself and what is important to me (SA = 4; A = 5; N = 1; D = 2)	3.9	1.08
Connective knowledge			Connective knowledge		
Increased my sense of connection to a wider world community (SA = 5; A = 4; N = 3)	4.1	0.83	Increased my sense of connection to a wider world community (SA = 1; A = 4; N = 3; D = 4)	3.8	1.02

Note. SD(1) = *strongly disagree*; D(2) = *disagree*; N(3) = *neutral*; A(4) = *agree*; SA(5) = *strongly agree*.

come to class during class time is essential for the overall success of this paradigm. Forging a successful collaboration with the community partner is a key ingredient to the overall success of this course.

This collaboration requires meeting the nonprofit organization before the course begins. Discussions include explaining the website development process, the expectations of the students, and the student roles. In addition, the logistics of when the Pace students can visit the community partner's location to gather information are explored. Last, discussions about when the community partner is expected to visit the class to review the students' prototype and when the final presentation is scheduled are included. Establishing clear guidelines and discussing dates are critical to the students gaining an enriched experience working with a real organization.

Students learning web design and development who do not have the opportunity to create a website for a real organization will not be well prepared. Their scope of employment will be limited. However, students who complete this course will have a competitive edge over students who have not. They will have the experience of interacting with a real client and developing a website for a real organization. This eService-Learning Hybrid II course provides the students with real-world experiences that they cannot obtain from a textbook, traditional lectures, and fictitious lab assignments. The eService-Learning Hybrid II model cultivates skill sets and on-the-job-training that is a valuable asset for job placement.

References

Cornell, R., & Martin, B. (1997). The role of motivation in web-based instruction. In B. A. Khan (Ed.), *Web-based instruction* (pp. 93–100). Englewood Cliffs, NJ: Educational Technology Publications.

Crabtree, R. D. (1998). Mutual empowerment in cross-cultural participatory development and service learning: Lessons in communication and social justice from projects in El Salvador and Nicaragua. *Journal of Applied Communication Research, 26*(2), 182–209.

Godfrey, P. C. (1999, December). Service-learning and management education: A call to action. *Journal of Management Inquiry,* 363–378.

Hazari, S. I., & Schnorr, D. (1999). Leveraging student feedback to improve teaching in web-based courses. *Technological Horizons in Education Journal, 26*(11), 30–38.

Rogers, C., & Freiberg, H. J. (1994). *Freedom to learn* (3rd ed.). New York, NY: Macmillan.

7

HYBRID III:
EACH ONE, TEACH ONE

Lessons From the Storm

Jean Strait

H urricane Katrina was the deadliest and most destructive Atlantic tropical cyclone of the 2005 Atlantic hurricane season. In New Orleans, the levees were designed for Category 3 hurricanes, but Katrina peaked at a Category 5, with winds up to 175 miles per hour. The storm surge from Katrina was 20 feet (6 meters) high. Hurricane Katrina affected over 15 million people, and the final death toll was at 1,836, primarily from Louisiana (1,577) and Mississippi (238). An estimated 80% of New Orleans was underwater, up to 20 feet deep in places. Hurricane Katrina caused $81 billion in property damages, but it is estimated that the total economic impact in Louisiana and Mississippi exceeded $150 billion. The region affected by the storm supported roughly 1 million nonfarm jobs, and hundreds of thousands of local residents are still unemployed as a result of the hurricane. More than 70 countries pledged monetary donations or other assistance after the hurricane (National Oceanic & Atmospheric Administration, 2009).

New Orleans has always been a unique and diverse city. Sitting 2 feet below sea level, the city has experienced hurricanes before but none as devastating as Katrina. Most of the damage and destruction occurred in the 9th Ward and 7th Ward of the city, the largest two wards in New Orleans and two of the poorest neighborhoods in the United States. The 9th Ward,

2.25 square miles, was washed away. The 7th Ward was destroyed when the London Avenue Canal was breached on both sides.

Institutional Contexts: Hamline University, Avalon High School, Dr. Martin Luther King Jr. Charter School for Science and Technology, and The Depot House

Hamline University, St. Paul, Minnesota

Hamline University, a medium-sized university in St. Paul, Minnesota, was one of the first institutions to respond to the tragedy and had first responders on the ground in New Orleans, helping the Dr. Martin Luther King Jr. Charter School for Science and Technology (previously known as the Martin Luther King Science and Technology Magnet School) teachers climb fences and try to salvage anything they could from the submerged school. The Hamline community sent over $20,000 in books, supplies, merchandise gift cards, food, and water to help with this effort within the first 2 weeks of the storm. This was the start of a multiyear partnership between Hamline, Dr. Martin Luther King Jr. Charter School for Science and Technology, The Depot House, and a host of community partners. Hamline professor Dr. Jean Strait began collaborations with several foundations and grantors. Initial funding came from Travelers Insurance and included St. Paul Avalon High School juniors and seniors. Over the course of the next 6 years, online mentoring and 13 face-to-face trips to New Orleans transformed the school, the community, and the participants. The program was named Each One, Teach One (EOTO; Strait & Jones, 2009).

Not only is Hamline the oldest university in Minnesota, it is rooted in the values and traditions of the United Methodist Church, which include a commitment to liberal education, civic engagement, social justice, and inclusive leadership and service. Every student completes an internship, collaborative research, a service-learning project, or field-based research (Strait & Saurer, 2004). Through the group's efforts, more than $500,000 was raised for community rebuilding, including the creation of an agricultural high school in the 9th district.

Avalon High School, St. Paul, Minnesota

Avalon High School was chosen as a partner because of the extensive commitment the school has for social justice and service-learning. Avalon has a college-prep focus, interdisciplinary seminars, project-based learning, and a technology component complemented by extensive training in ethics, conflict resolution, interpersonal and life skills, and active citizenship and community service. Junior- and senior-level students were selected on an application basis to work with EOTO during years 1 and 2. Although it was a founding partner, Avalon decided to create its own service-learning program after the second year of EOTO.

Dr. Martin Luther King Jr. Charter School for Science and Technology, 9th Ward, New Orleans

The New Orleans Public School system was wholly controlled by the Orleans Public School Board (OPSB) before Katrina devastated the city in August 2005, damaging or destroying more than 100 of the district's 128 school buildings. However, Katrina did not kill the New Orleans Public Schools. Fifty years prior to Hurricane Katrina's landfall, the OPSB-administered system was widely recognized as the lowest performing school district in Louisiana. When Katrina hit on August 29, 2005, 124 schools had already opened for the start of a new school year. According to data from the Times-Picayune newspaper, OPSB controlled 117 of those schools. The two worst hit areas were the 9th and 7th wards. Forth-five of the 117 schools were severely damaged or destroyed and most of these schools sat in the middle of the two ward (Times-Picayune, 2014). Students were displaced for the majority of the 2005–2006 school year. They simply did not go to school or have school elsewhere to attend. These schools did not reopen, in fact nine years later only 20 schools have been reopened in the devastated wards. Similar events occurred in Texas and Mississippi as well. Students who were lucky enough to relocate found themselves in districts that simply did not have the capacity to educate them. The districts that picked up the extra students lacked the essential classrooms, books and supplies. No one anticipated the level of post-traumatic stress disorder (PTSD) that these students would carry with them or the metal health issues that would ensue. "Schools with displaced students reported increases in disciplinary problems and a large unmet need for mental health counseling" (Southern Education Foundation, 2009, p. 5).

Dr. Martin Luther King Jr. Charter School for Science and Technology (MLK) was chosen as a partner because of its great need. Located in the 9th Ward, the neighborhood in which it is located was literally erased by Katrina. Many children were already 2 years behind academically before the storm hit. Today, MLK is seen as one of the highest achieving schools in Louisiana (see drkingcharterschool.org).

MLK was the first, and for many years the only, school that reopened in the 9th Ward in New Orleans. Many Hamline University students and staff were first responders to the school, hopping the school fence and wading through the mud to try to salvage what could be saved. Dr. Doris Hicks, principal of the school, was perhaps the most influential reason that MLK made it back on its feet so quickly. MLK was granted charter expansion, enabling the addition of a high-school-level program. In 2012, the first graduates completed the program.

The Depot House, New Orleans, Louisiana

Located in the Garden District, The Depot House at Madam Julia's is a historic landmark. Several volunteer groups worked on the old hotel while doing recovery work in New Orleans. Owned by Denny Hilton, also the owner of the St. Charles Guest House, The Depot has been featured in many movies, including *The Curious Case of Benjamin Button* (Kennedy, Marshall, & Chaffin, 2008). The EOTO team stayed at this location and helped make significant repairs on the buildings while in New Orleans.

Definition of *Hybrid III*: Instruction and Service Partially On-site and Online

As noted in chapter 2, Waldner, McGorry, and Widener's (2012) work depicting the types of eService-Learning place Hybrid III service-learning at the center of on-site and online instruction and service. Here, instruction and service are partially on-site and online (see Figure 7.1).

Figure 7.1 Four Emerging Types of eService-Learning

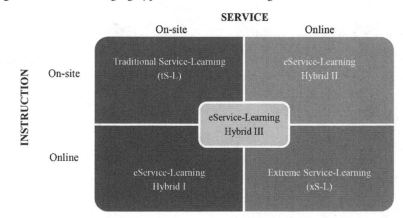

Note. Modified from Waldner et al. (2012).

The EOTO Model

The initial design for EOTO was to create a national-disaster-related education response model that could be replicated in any city in the United States. The program consisted of a joint online service-learning tutoring and mentoring program between Hamline University, Avalon High School, and MLK students in grades five through nine. The initial training of Hamline and Avalon tutors focused on citizenship skills (Partnership for 21st Century Skills, 2009), how to teach and involve students in a community project to reinforce their learning, and Internet mentoring and tutoring of students to assist with reading and study skills.

As the program grew, Avalon High School began offering different service-learning options for its students. By the fourth round of the class and trip, only Hamline students were taking part in tutoring and mentoring the New Orleans students. What was interesting was how many students stayed involved and held leadership roles throughout the year. I believed there was something happening to make the students want to be a part of this program year after year, and I wanted to find out what their thoughts were about the program. By the time we got to the fourth trip, 50% of the students had worked in EOTO for at least 2 years and wanted to be involved for a third year.

Program Goals

The project implementation team identified three major goals for the project:

1. *Student academic achievement in New Orleans:* improving the quality of education for New Orleans students and increasing their academic achievement by at least one grade level per academic year, encouraging students to finish high school, teaching students and teachers how to use technology, teaching students how to become civically engaged through service-learning projects in New Orleans with Hamline and Avalon students.
2. *Technology:* using technology to create a long-standing partnership with the New Orleans schools in order to help students receive the mentoring, tutoring, and support they need to be successful while also creating a much-needed connection to parents.
3. *Hamline student civic awareness:* teaching Hamline and Avalon students about community engagement and service-learning as part of becoming a global citizen with 21st-century skills.

Student Academic Achievement in New Orleans

The first two rounds of the program addressed the immediate rebuild of the 9th Ward. These students were already severely behind their peers by at least two grade levels before the storm. After Katrina, many missed 75% of that school year, putting them another year behind. Our challenge was to help bring these students to grade level without going too fast and risking dropout or shut down of the New Orleans students. The online component allowed students to ask questions and practice difficult subjects in a low-profile environment without the peer pressure or stigma that can be associated with asking for additional help.

Technology

When EOTO first started, we were limited in the types of technology available to us. Initially, we were concerned about privacy and underage issues of the New Orleans middle school students. As the lead partner, Hamline University was using Blackboard as its online course application software. Working with our institutional technology department, we created an individual specialized course shell that could be used by all participants. It was password protected to shield the middle school and high school students from any potential outside Internet influences. All Hamline and Avalon students completed a criminal background check to ensure additional safety. Initially during the first 2 years of the project, participants were fortunate that the Hamline University Safety and Security office could run the checks free of charge and electronically transmit the results to MLK, which also met New Orleans state requirements. Currently, students complete background checks online through the Minnesota State System, which costs $10 per student. This is considered a lab fee for the class, so university students can use financial aid to pay for it.

One of the first issues we encountered with technology was the limited availability the New Orleans middle school students had to the Internet. One computer lab was all the school had for all 450 students to use, and it was accessed through a sign-in basis only. The lab held 20 computers, and we were working with over 100 students. This meant that we needed a person on the ground in New Orleans to coordinate the times and connections for the middle school students. Consequently, Hamline and Avalon students utilized the chat room function of Blackboard where students could leave messages for one another and check them when access was available. This made the program slow in response to student needs.

One of the unintended results included the use of cell phones. All participants quickly discovered that texting questions or concerns to their mentor worked much faster than the system we had in place. If written help for homework was needed, then that work was submitted through the Blackboard process. Facebook and Twitter also became tools of choice for the students. They enjoyed sharing pictures and family stories. The texting was wonderful for our face-to-face encounters in New Orleans, as well as for participants' continued connections once Hamline and Avalon students returned to Minnesota. Today, EOTO participants routinely use mobile devices and hope to equip the middle school students with iPads.

Hamline Student Civic Awareness and Links to 21st-Century Skills

In addition to learning information and media literacy, all participants gained information, communication, and technology skills, which are considered essential 21st-century learning skills (Partnership for 21st Century Skills, 2013). Learning and innovation skills and life and career skills were also taught through EOTO.

Trip 4: Hamline Student Interviews

By the time round four of the project began, it was clear that Hamline students were forming long-term relationships with the community partners and students. Returning students naturally rose to leadership levels in the group. Many spoke of EOTO being like a family. This group was dedicated to creating positive change and growth in the 9th Ward.

Participant Demographics

The student makeup of this particular team included 33% international students, 56% Minnesota-born students, and 11% out-of-state students. The average age of the Hamline students was 20 years. Of the students, 62% were White, 17% were African American, 4% were Native American, and 17% were from various African countries. Although this was offered as an undergraduate option, 31% were nontraditional students, including one graduate student who had taken part in the first round as an undergraduate. The gender of the group was evenly split at 52% female and 48% male. Over half the students were in their junior year, and the other half of the group was evenly split between seniors (25%) and sophomores (25%). Socioeconomic makeup of the group consisted of lower class (33%), middle class (33%), and upper class (33%).

Interview Questions

Each participant was asked 10 questions during a 30-minute interview, which was recorded and transcribed. These transcriptions were then coded for potential themes, concepts, and behaviors. I wanted to find out what made the program important for the students, what they were able to identify that they were learning through these experiences, and whether they could identify any growth or changes in their own thinking and behaviors. With the Hybrid III model, the face-to-face trip was just as important as the tutoring and mentoring that was occurring online. I wanted to see if we could determine the essential components to see how the online work was influencing the face-to-face interaction and visa versa. The year 4 face-to-face trip also experienced a communication breakdown with one of the community partners that resulted in a shift of the group work.

The interview questions included the following:

1. Tell me about the program and trip.
2. Did you have any goals for the program?
3. Did anything unexpected happen?
4. What valuable learning experiences did you have?
5. Did you learn anything about communication?
6. Did you have any fears about the program?
7. Did you learn anything about diversity through the program?
8. What do you think the government could or should do about the issues in New Orleans?
9. What did you learn about leadership?
10. If you were to speak with funders about this program, what would you tell them? Why should this program be funded (or not funded)?

Analysis: Themes

Research shows us that students who participate in service-learning strengthen their soft skills such as critical thinking, empathy, and relationship building (Eyler & Giles, 1999; Leimer, Yue, & Rogulkin, 2009; Moely, McFarland, Miron, Mercer, & Ilustre, 2002; Simons & Cleary, 2006). In their future careers, participants have to be able to sell ideas, set goals, articulate viewpoints, and communicate effectively. They also have to be able to identify leadership and navigate diverse populations.

Students received training before the online component of the program began, which included learning about the history and background of New Orleans, Hurricane Katrina, poverty, learned helplessness, post-traumatic stress disorder (PTSD), and addiction; learning how to mentor and tutor students and how to encourage and motivate them; learning how to use technology to connect with students; creating and organizing a service-learning project; and learning how to write grants and how to speak with potential partners and funders about project ideas. Student leaders each round worked with the faculty leaders to select training materials and suggest guest speakers to discuss needed topics.

As could be expected, Hamline students who had participated in the program for 3 or 4 years were more able to articulate their answers and showed great conviction in doing so. Students participating in their first and second year were shocked by their face-to-face experience in New Orleans and related most of their interview to deconstructing that shock response.

Year 1 and Year 2 Participants' Responses

Few beginning participants were able to articulate personal goals for their participation in EOTO. Over 33% said they had no idea what they were getting into and were shocked by the face-to-face trip. Their responses were more general when answering questions about learning experiences and potential funders, whereas they were very specific about their own communication, fears, and leadership. Many noted the "welcoming" atmosphere of the community and how that wasn't the case in St. Paul. Diversity was discussed from within the EOTO group instead of the people they were working with in the partnerships.

Communication

I was shy, but those guys pulled me in. We didn't know each other before, and now we talk like family.

I had to learn to get out of my shell.

I made some friends, and I opened up to . . . [other participants]. I trust these [EOTO] folks more now that we have had this experience.

Fears

I was worried about the crime rate. I didn't want to get hurt or robbed. New Orleans has a very high crime rate. I was worried I wouldn't be accepted.

I thought we would be rejected, but we were so welcomed . . . never a time I didn't feel appreciated.

The training sessions washed away all my fears . . . they made all the difference.

I was worried that the kids would be damaged forever. I was afraid I didn't or wouldn't be able to make a difference.

I was worried about working with the kids.

I was worried about the chaos and what could be done. . . . Can we make a difference?

Leadership

> [This person] was a powerful leader, flexible and accessible, funny and relaxed.
>
> Don't worry about what others think; do what is right.
>
> You have to step up if you see a need.
>
> [This person] had character, and I wanted that too.
>
> It [leadership] can go a long way, and even if you feel you failed, you are still a leader for it; you did your best. . . . You have done so much, and this is just one little thing.

Diversity

Year 1 and year 2 students had less experience working with diversity. Participants' comments included the following:

> I learned a lot about diversity from our student leaders and our team.
>
> We were from all over.
>
> I was surprised by how well we got along even though we were so different.
>
> I met people I normally wouldn't hang out with, and yet I totally bonded with these people. They know who I am and like me anyway. We moved beyond stereotypes. . . . Everyone doesn't deserve to get to know me.
>
> It doesn't matter who you are or what you look like. . . . We were all equal; it didn't matter down there. I didn't know [this person was] Black until I met them face-to-face.

Year 3 and Year 4 Participants' Responses

Hamline student mentors in years 3 and 4 were able to deconstruct different issues and problems. They could see multiple sides of an issue and multiple layers or complexity of a problem. Goals for this group were very well defined, with a clear focus on communication, careers, and leadership. These students were able to analyze their own personal strengths and weaknesses. Hamline students at this level were also able to "sell" the program to the community partners and potential funders. Terms like *relational trust*, *PTSD*, and *cognitive dissonance* appeared in their interviews 82% more than they did in the interviews with year 1 and year 2 mentors. Links to career application skills were reported by all participants (100%) at this level. Examples of each are provided next.

Communication

I can communicate with any stakeholder in this project whether it is a student, a community partner, a peer, or a teacher. I realized that we communicate indirectly even when we don't consciously know we are. That's what professionalism is about, communicating through presence.

It [communication] was a lot more challenging, and it still didn't guarantee the message got across. . . . [This person] didn't know what to do and when to do it, which made things very frustrating.

The community trusted us more, and we started to have a great relationship each time we returned to the city. The same thing happened online; students could ask for help, and we'd be there. They came to trust we would be there and be able to help.

Communication was critical, and if we all weren't on the same page, this wasn't going to work.

I learned that for planning, not only was reliable communication needed but reliable people to communicate with. . . . If I couldn't depend on the people I was working with, then no matter how well I communicated, the planning wouldn't get done.

Career and Leadership

I wanted to work in the school. In my career I will have to deal with alcoholism, bipolar disorder, and lack of resources to take on basic needs. Where does social services fit on this? Where is the money to treat PTSD? [this student] needed meds to improve their cognitive functioning.

I wanted to work with the community again. Our presence motivated the community to get involved. I faced my worst fear and lived through it. . . . I know now that I can do anything. Leadership is a balancing act, and you have to work to find that balance . . . when you do, it's magic. Our strengths and weaknesses balanced each other out.

I learned full-blown leadership. I had to think on my feet. I never knew how much background and planning work needed to be done. From getting food, to planning activities . . . even getting supplies. I am self-confident, knowledgeable, and not afraid to speak up. I realize the importance of communication with all stakeholders and that professionalism is key. You need to know how things should be done. As an ESL teacher, when conflict happens, I know how to handle this.

Diversity

I learned there is diversity within personalities. We started to always question why people were the way they were and not stereotype. This is where deep impactful education occurs, where you learn about people. The real world is not in the classroom; the real world is my classroom.

People act differently in different situations, and you can't apply how you would react in every situation. At the end of the day, you really don't know.

Discussion

The blended hybrid model provided participants with the opportunity to have long-term connections to students and practice professional skills needed when working with community partners. Both online and face-to-face work was essential for deeper level processing, self-assessment, and greater connection to careers and life skills. Participants were better equipped to handle multiple layers of analysis and the complexities of a problem. For example, when the course shell (Blackboard) was not functioning the way the leadership team had intended, the student leaders were quick to switch to texting and Twitter to get the job done. Not only were these technologies quicker and more easily accessible, they allowed for more informal exchanges of information. Students were less anxious about getting homework help. Mentors were more accessible. Less content formatting was needed on the Blackboard site when texting and Twitter were offered as alternatives.

When mentors had more face-to-face experience with the community partners, they were better able to advocate for the program with funders and state regulators. When mentors worked with students online, fewer personality conflicts occurred. Taking away the face-to-face work initially helped to strengthen mentor–student communication and eliminate any potential bias. Putting it back in for the trip to New Orleans eliminated the cognitive dissonance so often associated with issues that occur outside one's own circle of experience.

Conclusions and Recommendations

Use a Hybrid III model when

- a project is trying to reach across long distances for longer periods of time;
- you have the technology capable of providing quick, cheap connections to community partners so communication can happen often and fast; or
- high levels of anxiety are present in one or more of the partners. (The elimination of the initial face-to-face can help partners relax and get to know one another so that deeper levels of processing and growth can occur.)

Since EOTO began 6 years ago, houses have been rebuilt and people have returned to their homes, but a great deal has been left undone. Bureaucratic red tape continues to slow the process. Only 76 homes have been built by Brad Pitt's foundation, despite the wealth and influence behind its work. Several city blocks have been taken over by vegetation, bringing snakes and other unwanted animals into an already fragile environment. The old and the poor have little they can do to improve their living conditions. PTSD continues to be at one of the highest levels in New Orleans. Many of the children EOTO first worked with have graduated from high school this year and are now moving into the workforce. If they were at MLK, they are graduating successfully; if not, then many are not graduating at all. The only difference was EOTO.

Although this program has been a success, there are many other cities and countries that could benefit from the replication of this Hybrid III model. Recently a cyclone the size of Hurricane Katrina with the power of Hurricane Andrew hit the coast of India, displacing over 500,000 people. More funding and resources could be directed to creating larger scale EOTO programs that could work with partners and students all over the world. As a three-time EOTO student leader said,

> If we don't do it, who will? It [the EOTO program] teaches us empathy and life skills. Removal of emotion removes the power to act; we need that to help others. We have a civic responsibility to do so. I never once thought about those people in New Orleans, now that I have been there, I can't stop. . . . My first student group is 18, and we still text each other today. [A student] is coming to my wedding! She's like a little sister.

References

Eyler, J., & Giles, D. E. Jr. (1999). *Where's the learning in service-learning.* San Francisco, CA: Jossey-Bass.

Kennedy, K., Marshall, F., & Chaffin, C (Producers), Fincher, D. (Director). (2008). *The curious case of Benjamin Button.* United States: Paramount.

Leimer, C., Yue, H., & Rogulkin, D. (2009, June). Does service learning help students succeed? Assessing the effects of service learning at California State University-Fresno. *Institutional Research, Assessment and Planning,* 1–18.

Moely, B. E., McFarland, M., Miron, D., Mercer, S., & Ilustre, V. (2002). Changes in college students' attitudes and intentions for civic involvement as a function of service-learning experiences. *Michigan Journal of Community Service Learning, 9*(1), 18–26.

National Oceanic & Atmospheric Administration. (2009). *Digital elevation models of New Orleans, Louisiana: Procedures, data sources and analysis* (NOAA Technical Memorandum NESDIS NGDC-49). Boulder, CO: National Geophysical Data Center, Marine Geology and Geophysics Division.

Partnership for 21st Century Skills. (2009). *P2 framework definitions.* Retrieved from http://www.p21.org/storage/documents/P21_Framework_Definitions.pdf

Partnership for 21st Century Skills. (2013). *Framework for 21st century learning.* Retrieved from http://www.p21.org/

Simons, L., & Cleary, B. (2006). The influence of service learning on students' personal and social development. *College Teaching, 54*(4), 307–320.

Southern Education Foundation. (2009). *New Orleans schools four years after Katrina: A lingering federal responsibility.* Retrieved from: http://www.southern education.org/getattachment/2bfd6ee2-810f-4785-8d6f-b9ee305228f1/New-Orleans-Schools-Four-Years-After-Katrina-A-Lin.aspx

Strait, J., & Jones, J. (2009). *Each One, Teach One program.* Retrieved May 20, 2010, from http://www.eric.ed.gov/ERICWebPortal/detail?accno=EJ853211

Strait, J., & Sauer, T. (2004). *Constructing experiential learning for online courses: The birth of e-service.* Retrieved May 20, 2010, from http://www.educause.edu/EDUCAUSE+Quarterly/EDUCAUSEQuarterlyMagazineVolume/ConstructingExperientialLearning/157274

Waldner, L. S., McGorry, S. Y., & Widener, M. C. (2012). E-service-learning: The evolution of service-learning to engage a growing online student population. *Journal of Higher Education Outreach and Engagement, 16*(2), 123–150.

8

HYBRID IV: EXTREME eSERVICE-LEARNING

Online Service-Learning in an Online Business Course

Sue McGorry

Imagine trudging through a community in southern Brazil, or building a schoolhouse in that same Brazilian community. Now imagine conducting a project to measure the success of or to communicate that Amazon experience completely online. Welcome Extreme eService-Learning to the pedagogical platform. Service-learning has gained popularity in academia as a pedagogical tool because it facilitates social responsibility while reinforcing academic learning. Service-learning typically involves a community activity or project that links real-world or hands-on experience to course concepts. The projects usually include some form of personal reflection, enabling students to consider the meaning of their civic participation and its effects on both themselves and the community.

Also growing in popularity is online learning. Consider the following statistics: 18% of undergraduate students are predicted to receive 80% or more of their education via online courses by 2013 ("Growth of Distance Learning," 2013). In addition, there was a 150% increase in the number of students selecting distance-learning courses as a part of their regular college curriculum between 1998 and 2008 ("Growth of Distance Learning," 2013). Fifty percent of college presidents believe that 10 years from now the majority of their students will take online classes (Parker, Lenhart, & Moore, 2011).

Definition

When eService-Learning is done in an online course, both the course and the service are conducted online. This type of eService-Learning is called Extreme eService-Learning. There is no on-site component (McGorry, 2012; Waldner, McGorry, & Widener, 2010) to this type of project. How can this be? Isn't the premise of service-learning an opportunity for students to engage with the external community and an opportunity for the academic institution to develop a long-term ongoing partnership with an external community organization?

In a traditional service-learning project, students should learn the practical applications of their studies, and they should also become actively contributing citizens and community members through the service they perform (National Service-Learning Clearing House, 2013). This too can be achieved in an online service-learning experience.

In this chapter, the components of a successful Extreme eService-Learning experience are presented. This experience demonstrates how eService-Learning is integrating meaningful community service with instruction and reflection in order to enrich the learning experience, teach civic responsibility, and strengthen communities through online instruction.

Academic institutions should regard eService-Learning in online courses as the opportunity to transform both service-learning and online learning. Extreme eService-Learning can free service-learning from geographical constraints and create a powerful engagement tool in online learning (Waldner et al., 2010).

General Considerations

Instructors need to consider the learning venue in developing online service-learning projects and outcomes. There are several critical factors exclusive to the Extreme eService-Learning experience that must be addressed: time frame of the course, student and partner organization availability, course technology to support the project, and partner logistics. These factors will directly impact the type of project conducted and how it can be managed online. The following are project ideas that could be facilitated well online:

- Marketing research to understand a new audience for a service
- Planning and development of an online training program to teach an audience about personal finance
- Planning, development, and delivery of a counseling program delivered online to at-risk populations

- Development of a fund-raising plan for an organization
- Development and delivery of an online language training tool
- Development of a promotional plan for a local CSA (Community Supported Agriculture)

Time Frame

Although a traditional course may be 15 weeks in length, a condensed course taught online or a course serving an adult population may be only 6 to 8 weeks in length. In selecting a project to facilitate course learning outcomes, the instructor must choose a project that would be well managed in that time frame. When considering time frames for service-learning projects, the instructor might want to consider the course level (graduate students often work full-time) and the population of students enrolled in the course (adult learners, many of whom have additional responsibilities). Adult learners are the target audience in many online courses ("Growth of Distance Learning," 2013), so the instructor must consider these issues when selecting a project topic.

Student and Partner Availability

Again, this alludes to the fact that working adults often may be the participants in an Extreme eService-Learning experience, and the project must be manageable within a shorter time frame and in a venue that fits their work schedule. The partner organization must commit to availability that provides students with the opportunity to successfully complete a project. Because of the various student populations (graduate students, adult students, evening students, etc.), it is helpful to work with a community partner who can provide a member of its team to be available after normal business hours to assist the student population with a project.

Course Tools

An Extreme eService-Learning experience requires technology that facilitates seamless communication for students and the partner organizations. This must include chat with either audio or video capability. E-mail and discussion boards established by the team are also critical, as they enable the team to communicate asynchronously yet keep documents and ideas centrally located.

McGorry (2012) described a course where business students developed a promotional campaign for a newly formed nonprofit organization. The students were tasked with learning the history of the organization, understanding the principals and the newly formed board, and exploring the market that the organization was attempting to reach. In this case study, students employed e-mail, synchronous chats with the client organization and with their own team members, file exchange, and discussion boards to address course content. Students reported feeling engaged and challenged, and they believed these technological tools were essential to course and project communication.

Partner Logistics

In the Extreme eService-Learning model, a variety of projects may be successfully facilitated. It is important for the instructor to consider the following limitations and issues specific to the project deliverable or "product" that may change the dynamics of a project. An academic institution could consider traditional service-learning projects that may require fieldwork as long as some of the class members are local to the area. If this is not possible, depending on the structure of the semester (quarter, trimester) other projects may be developed based on specific time frames.

Community partners in traditional service-learning efforts tend to be nonprofit organizations that in some way contribute to communities (Bringle & Hatcher, 1996). Partner organizations must feel comfortable with the online venue and communicating with students electronically whether through e-mail, discussion boards, online chats, or a combination of these methods. The instructor can include the partner organization as a "student participant" enrolled in the course electronically. This is important to mention, because in a completely online course, only students and the instructor would have access to the course server. In the case of Extreme eService-Learning, it would be beneficial to all parties involved to have access to the server. Course material, partner organization documentation, and any recorded chats or discussion boards would be accessible to all. This is critical to the success of the project. Students can then readily access the partner organization when necessary. This also enables the students to arrange and conduct private chat sessions with the partner organization at their convenience without intervention from the instructor. Some examples of Extreme eService-Learning projects include one provided in Burton (2003), who facilitated an online service-learning project for students developing websites for the sale of items in a village in Guatemala. Malvey, Hamby, and Fottler (2006) taught a finance course online with a service-learning project that created a zero-based budget for a local county health department. Waldner, Roberts, Widener, and Sullivan (2011) evaluated an Extreme eService-Learning course that provided two valuable services for Fulton County, Georgia. Students researched best practices and did a policy analysis on health disparity issues of concern to the county, such as infant mortality or childhood obesity.

Creating an Extreme eService-Learning Course

In this project, students are enrolled as graduate students in a marketing management course in the business school. Although this is a required course, students have the option to complete this course either online or in the traditional classroom. The service-learning component is not required of students in the program. The institution is a liberal arts Christian institution, so the service-learning component of the program is well aligned with the institution's mission.

Relationships with partner organizations are created and developed up to 6 months to a year in advance. Organizations may be local to the academic institution's physical location, or projects can include locations abroad or in another area of the country.

Prior to consultation with a prospective client organization, the instructor should review the mission and history of the organization. Once a project idea has been discussed, the instructor and partner must determine if the course outcomes can be aligned with the organization's needs. Once this is ascertained, the instructor can present a preliminary project outline with goals to the partner organization. This assists the client organization as well in determining the possible needs of the students going forward: Will the students need access to organizational records? If so, how will these documents be shared? Will there be one particular individual in the organization who can provide a communication venue, or will the students need to communicate with several members of the organization?

A detailed project outline must be developed in order to provide students with structured guidance and project deliverables. The outline must reflect the course content and be available within the first week of the course. This enables students to manage their time ahead and determine how they might like to structure their own team online sessions.

Students proceed with the course material as presented online. The instructor makes online lectures and material available in text format. Chat sessions are scheduled biweekly (or more often if indicated by the instructors or students) to provide students with a hands-on time with other students and the instructor and partner organization.

From week 1, students are required to maintain an online journal about the service-learning project. These are typically organized by week. The instructor may provide guided questions so that students know what to address in the journal entries. Students are invited to comment on project topics, findings, team dynamics, challenges, and other issues relative to the project. Students are reminded that these are confidential journal entries and will not be shared with other students.

In week 2, a representative from the partner organization joins the entire class in an online chat session in order to provide a framework for the project to the students. This may include some historical background about the organization and the project. This creates a true sense of empowerment for the students and also creates a sense of confidence about addressing the project issues.

During week 3, students are presented with online resources to support their projects. In the business discipline, this would include a review of the literature, as well as other statistical and secondary data that would be useful for the project. This is to prepare students to address whichever issues face the organization in achieving the project outcomes.

Instructors should arrange to have online librarians from the home institution join the students and instructor in this session. The librarians have access to the project outline and materials prior to the session so that they may provide an overview of resources that are germane to the project topic. This also provides an opportunity for the librarian to customize the session by course and project.

Midway through the course, the same representative from the partner organization will join all course students again for an online chat. The representative may have been communicating continually with students and student teams, but this open forum provides all the students with another perspective on the project and an opportunity to ask questions now that more information has been gathered. All of these sessions are recorded in an effort to allow those who may not be available to listen to the chats at their convenience. Students can then post questions to the project discussion board if anything needs clarification.

As the students approach week 10, the focus of the course turns exclusively to the final project. The students are no longer required to complete weekly assignments, and the course readings and lectures are complete. At this time, the instructor will create discussion boards by team, usually four to six teams per course section. Student teams are then invited to post their final recorded presentations so that all course members can view them. If it's possible, another variation on this model is to have all students and partner organization representatives online simultaneously to present final results. This typically generates productive discussion among all team members and the partner organization.

LaSalle University Model

In this case study, the Extreme eService-Learning project is conducted with MBA students online at LaSalle University, a private liberal arts university in the northeastern United States. There are approximately 2,500 traditional and continuing education students enrolled in both undergraduate and graduate programs at the university. Students are predominantly White (87%), with a 45% male and 55% female student population. The 12-week course is a marketing course required of all MBA students. The number of students in the course during this semester is 18. All 18 students participated in the Extreme eService-Learning project.

The partner organization is a newly formed nonprofit organization. The organization is named after a fallen officer and is dedicated to education, fostering lifelong learning in public safety, and enhancing the community's awareness of public service. The foundation's goal is to work with community members, local educators, public officials, and law enforcement agencies and to mentor relationships between positive adult role models and children, preparing them for responsible citizenship. The goal of the project was that students would develop a promotional plan for the organization.

Lessons Learned

Students participated in a focus group to identify issues that were critical to the success of the eService-Learning experience. This was done at the end of the course.

Initial Meeting With Client

In focus groups, the majority of the students noted that the initial chat with the client was extremely important in developing rapport and understanding the issues to be addressed in the project. At this meeting, students were introduced to the organization, provided with material relative to the organizations and their client, and invited to ask questions about the organization, the history, and the issues related to the project. Students overwhelmingly agreed that this meeting was essential to their level of relationship with the partner.

Commitment From Client to Be Available Online: Chats, Boards, E-mail

As the project progressed, students were encouraged to communicate with the partner in order to obtain project data and to understand the client organization and its needs. To stay in contact with students, the partner organization participated in periodic chat sessions; communicated via discussion boards, phone, and e-mail; and invited students to on-site visits. However, students indicated that lapses in communication with the partner organization were troublesome as the majority of students believed that regular communication with the client was absolutely critical to the project's success. This issue should be investigated more closely, as reports of noncommunication may be misconstrued. For example, some students waited until a few days before project material was due and would e-mail the clients expecting responses within 24 hours. This should not be considered "problematic" communication.

Electronic Resources (Library Databases, Websites, etc.) and Meetings With the Librarian

An information librarian was available specifically for the class project to support students' information needs. The librarian held an introductory session to provide direction and guidance to resources that would be useful specifically for the client's project. The librarian reviewed the project outline prior to providing the class with resources specific to the project. Fifteen of the 18 students indicated that the resources and guidance provided by the university's information services were indispensable. The librarian was available both live and online for all projects and would assist students throughout the semester with specific data needs.

Instructor Availability

The instructor was available not only via e-mail and on campus but also online for additional office hours on a weekly basis to accommodate project information needs. In addition, students were invited to meet periodically with the instructor in order to discuss project issues. Sixteen of the 18 students indicated that these meetings were very important to the project's progress. Often the instructor was needed to assist with the management of team issues.

Essential Tools

Students had Chatware (both full class and private with audio and video), discussion boards, file exchange, and group e-mail available via the institution's server (Blackboard) for the course. All of the students stated that these tools were essential to facilitate communication and enable collaboration on the project. These tools are not always applied in an online course setting; however, in this eService-Learning experience, students believed that these tools were important to the success of the project.

Reflection

As student reflection is an important component of the service-learning experience, students were required to maintain weekly journal entries. Although students complained about the amount of work in the first few weeks of the course, final journal submissions indicated that students had been provided with more opportunities to think about their learning experience and what exactly they had learned in the project. Students also contemplated the team experience they had encountered, as well as leadership issues. Although the instructor initially had provided a set of basic questions the students were to address each week, students began to express their experiences in more detail and provided more information about the team project throughout the semester. Seventy-one percent of students believed the journals contributed to better project understanding.

Students wrote reflections including the following:

I learned a good deal from the team experience in this project.

I did not realize how much time I would need to spend reviewing the history and past experience of the organization.

I think this experience of writing about our project is very valuable.

I would have liked the client to be more responsive and respond to our questions more quickly.

I feel as if I earned great practical business experience and learned how to work with a client from this project!

Limitations

Client Relationships

For some students, service-learning may be more difficult to facilitate online, as many desire the tangibility of face-to-face meetings. In this model, to develop a stronger more cohesive relationship between the client organization and the student team, the instructor must structure communication within the course platform to include a variety of tools to support multiple modes of communication. Students were able to communicate with the client organization via e-mail, discussion boards, and chat sessions. Even though the instructor provided all resources and communication online in this case study, there were a few students local to the partner site who still insisted on visiting the partner off-line.

Teamwork Online

In the business discipline, teamwork is often used to facilitate course learning because it is a critical transferable business skill that successful business students must understand and be comfortable with. In addition, many service-learning projects require the use of "team" projects (Govekar & Rishi, 2007). In fact, according to Eyler and Giles (1999), 40% of their survey respondents indicated that learning to work with other people was one of the important lessons they gained in their service-learning experience. From a business perspective, this is a critical skill to be developed in a service-learning experience (whether online or in a traditional classroom setting). It enables students to become professional and responsible and learn important negotiation and communication skills.

Teamwork can be accomplished via discussion boards, e-mail, and chat sessions. However, there can be difficulties attempting to facilitate synchronous teamwork because of differences in time zones and work and personal schedules. The instructor for this course established a number of modalities. E-mail was set up so that students had access to individual personal e-mail, but they also can easily e-mail team members and the client organization. Team members were not always available to be online simultaneously, so the chat function was sometimes used for private chats among team members or with the partner organization. Students had the option, through group functions, to set up private chat sessions between their client and team members (versus whole class chats in the public chat course setting). Often students wanted the privacy a group chat provided so as not to share all of their information with the entire class.

Sense of Community

Often in a service-learning setting, students report feeling a strong sense of community because they are actually physically working out in the community (Malvey et al., 2006). In this particular model, and in many business projects, students may be developing "behind-the-scenes" material that supports a business effort in the community. So, for example, instead of dishing out a meal in a food pantry line or digging trenches for irrigation of a farm, a student may develop a promotional campaign for a nonprofit organization. In this particular type of project, the sense of community and civic responsibility that students should be acquiring may not be similar to a more traditional physical service-learning experience. Future research should compare the traditional and online service-learning experience in achieving civic and community experience outcomes.

Summary

The future of Extreme eService-Learning is clear: It has arrived and will continue to grow and evolve as institutions adopt and explore new technologies that will enable them to meet the educational needs of a changing market.

Institutions cannot exclude online learners from this new pedagogical model. It would be a significant disadvantage to online learners and to academic institutions and their prospective partners not to use eService-Learning pedagogy.

Academic institutions must continue to experiment with a variety of partner institutions and new projects that stretch the boundaries of the models discussed in this chapter. For example, eService-Learning can create opportunities that would have never before existed, like allowing a student in Iowa Falls, Iowa, to participate in a planning commission study in Philadelphia, Pennsylvania. Likewise, a student in the city of Zaragoza, Spain, can be transported to the peanut fields of Tifton, Georgia, to develop a crop rotation plan in an agricultural management course. With Extreme eService-Learning, the service and learning possibilities are endless!

References

Bringle, R. G., & Hatcher, J. A. (1996). Implementing service-learning in higher education. *Journal of Higher Education, 67*(2), 221–239.

Burton, E. (2003). Distance learning and service-learning in the accelerated format. *New Directions for Adult and Continuing Education, 2003*(97), 63–72.

Eyler, J., & Giles, D. E. (1999). *Where's the learning in service-learning?* San Francisco, CA: Jossey-Bass.

Govekar, M. A., & Rishi, M. (2007). Service-learning: Bringing real-world education into the B-school classroom. *Journal of Education for Business, 83*(1), 3–10.

Growth of distance learning. (2013). Retrieved April 1, 2013, from http://edtechreview .in/news/news/data-statistics/138-growth-distance-learning-highered

Malvey, D. M., Hamby, E. F., & Fottler, M. D. (2006). E-service-learning: A pedagogic innovation for healthcare management education. *Journal of Health Administration Education, 33*(2), 181–198.

McGorry, S. (2012). No significant difference in service-learning online. *Journal of Asynchronous Learning Networks, 16*(4), 45–54.

Parker, K., Lenhart, A., & Moore, K. (2011). *The digital revolution and higher education.* Pew Internet and American Life Project. Retrieved from http:// pewinternet.org/Reports/2011/College-presidents/Summary.aspx

Toncar, M. F., Reid, J. S., & Anderson, C. E. (2005). Exploratory study to measure the validity of the SELEB scale. *Journal of the Academy of Business and Economics, 5*(1), 173–179.

Waldner, L. S., McGorry, S. Y., & Widener, M. C. (2012). E-service-learning: The evolution of service-learning to engage a growing online student population. *Journal of Higher Education Outreach and Engagement, 16*(2), 123–150.

Waldner, L., Roberts, K., Widener, M., & Sullivan, B. (2011). Serving up justice: Fusing service-learning and social equity in the public administration classroom. *Journal of Public Affairs Education, 17*(2), 209–232.

9

MIXED HYBRID: HYBRID I AND HYBRID III eSERVICE-LEARNING

Investigating the Influence of Online Components on Service-Learning Outcomes at the University of Georgia

Paul H. Matthews

This volume and other recent works (e.g., Dailey-Hebert, Donnelli-Sallee, & DiPadova-Stocks, 2008; Kenworthy-U'Ren, 2008; Matthews, 2011, 2012; Post, 2008; Waldner, McGorry, & Widener, 2012) reflect a growing interest in how components of online instruction merge with service-learning and the potential benefits that accrue from the resultant eService-Learning. Most authors have concluded that online learning "is not only compatible with but enhances and extends the aims of service-learning" (Dailey-Hebert et al., 2008, p. 1), with a range of perceived benefits including enhanced reflection opportunities, simplified time and content management, better preparation for community engagement, and so on. However, few of these assertions have been investigated in anything other than case study reports (e.g., Bailey & Card, 2009; Bennett & Green, 2001). Thus, additional research is warranted "to compare the outcomes of eService-Learning to those in traditional service-learning experiences, especially in areas related to performance differences in learning outcomes, civic engagement, professional development, and more" (Waldner et al., 2012, p. 126). In this chapter, I draw on data from multiple iterations of a campus-wide end-of-semester service-learning student survey to investigate the influence of online components on student learning outcomes in service-learning course work.

Institutional Context: The University of Georgia

The institutional setting for this study is the University of Georgia (UGA), a large (>34,000-student), public, high-research, land- and sea-grant institution located in Athens, a medium-sized yet high-poverty city in northeast Georgia. UGA has been recognized annually by the President's Higher Education Community Service Honor Roll for its student and faculty involvement in service and service-learning, and it received the Community Engagement classification from the Carnegie Foundation in 2010. While service-learning course work is not a university-wide requirement, UGA's Office of Service-Learning (established in 2005) provides professional development and resources to support faculty, students, and community partners interested in engaging in academic service-learning. A substantial and growing number of courses that incorporate service-learning are offered each year; for instance, over 360 course sections were available during 2011–2012, reaching over 6,200 students at the undergraduate, graduate, and professional levels across all of UGA's schools and colleges.[1]

Although UGA established an Office of Online Learning in August 2012, the university historically has had few fully online courses or programs available. For instance, prior to the establishment of that office, only about 230 courses were institutionally identified with the "E" suffix (Sherry Clouser, personal communication, July 27, 2012) used to indicate that at least 50% of the course is taught online. However, every course loaded into the university's course registration system automatically generates a "shell" within UGA's online support platform, presently called "eLearning Commons (eLC)", via the Blackboard Learning System Vista Enterprise Edition. There is no requirement for instructors to use eLC, so each instructor can choose whether to use this platform, for instance, to host readings or content modules, track grades and assignments, collect student reflective writings and assignments, create chats, and/or perform similar functions. During the 2011–2012 academic year, about 3,000 sections each semester actually populated these shells with at least some online content (Clouser, personal communication, July 27, 2012).

Waldner et al. (2012; see also Waldner, chapter 2 of this volume) conceptualized different ways in which eService-Learning can be structured, primarily based on which course elements are online and which are done in person or on-site. From the UGA Office of Service-Learning's internal tracking of courses, in the past several years only a single service-learning course has carried the "E" suffix, indicating a primarily online instructional delivery, while many instructors of "regular" service-learning classes do incorporate some level of tools within eLCs for content and assignment management. Additionally, though less common, some instructors and even community partner agencies have also reported using online tools to help prepare students for engagement with the community, to recruit or track service activities, and for similar supports. Based on these data, to the extent that eService-Learning is undertaken at our institution, it primarily entails a blending of face-to-face service activities with instruction that utilizes some online tools.[2] Thus, Waldner et al.'s Hybrid III model characterized by instruction or service partially on-site and partially online seems the most prevalent form of eService-Learning on our campus. However, at least one course fits the Hybrid I (instruction online, service on-site) model, described next.

Hybrid I: An Online Service-Learning Tutoring Course

Beginning in 2005–2006, I developed and taught a service-learning course through the College of Education designed to engage UGA students from a range of majors (mostly outside the College of Education) in after-school community and school-based tutoring programs supporting the academic, social, and literacy development of Latino English-language-learning elementary and middle school students. As I described more fully elsewhere (Matthews, 2011), to minimize some of the logistical and scheduling challenges of the course, I converted the instructional component to fully online as of the spring 2008 semester, while retaining the on-site service components (20–60 hours over the semester), arranged by the students with the community partners based on their schedules and needs. After moving from the College of Education to the UGA Office of Service-Learning in 2010, another instructor in the College of Education took over the course, keeping the format and content the same.

A qualitative analysis of student course-ending reflections (Matthews, 2011) found that students identified the online content as helpful for the community-based tutoring experience, affirmed the value of the flexible scheduling allowed by the blended format, and appreciated receiving online feedback from the instructor and their peers on their reflective journaling. Students also commented on the challenges of keeping up with online content in the absence of a regularly scheduled meeting time, and some suggested a face-to-face meeting would be helpful.

Survey Instrument

Data for this chapter's investigation come from multiple semesters of an end-of-course student questionnaire on service-learning courses and their outcomes and impacts. The survey was originally developed by UGA's Office of Service-Learning and Office of Institutional Effectiveness in 2007, based on the Service-Learning Benefit (SELEB) scale (Toncar, Reid, Burns, Anderson, & Nguyen, 2006), the Community-Based Learning–Student Survey (Gelmon, Holland, Driscoll, Spring, & Kerrigan, 2001), along with institutional variables of interest; it was piloted, administered for several semesters, and modified subsequently. The current (revised Fall 2009) version includes 67 items requesting demographic information; open-ended and Likert-type responses gauging the kinds, quantity, and impacts of the community-based activities; and open-ended comments for the specific course and instructor.[3] The UGA Office of Service-Learning administers the voluntary survey at the end of each semester to participants in UGA service-learning courses. Course instructors sign up their classes, and students are e-mailed a link with a request to participate; the survey is hosted in Qualtrics, an online survey tool. Survey data were exported each semester, then reviewed and imported into IBM/SPSS Statistics 21.0 for analysis.

Participants

The overall data for this chapter's study are based on 10 (Fall 2009 through Fall 2012) administrations of this survey (65 unique courses, 131 course sections in 30 departments, including undergraduate, graduate, and professional courses). Some 1,994 students elected to participate, representing 49.7% of available students in these courses.[4] Similar to service-learning's demographics nationally, the majority of respondents were female (69.1%) and White (72.1%) and indicated no previous experience in service-learning (56.7%). Their median age was 20, and most respondents were undergraduates: 43.2% were seniors (fourth or fifth year), 22.4% juniors, 11.2% sophomores, and 9.2% freshmen; 9.7% were in master's programs, 1.1% in doctoral programs, and 3.3% in professional programs (e.g., pharmacy).

The most common service activities reported were educational activities, tutoring, and consultation; at UGA, both indirect and direct service activities are applicable for academic service-learning, and there is no university-specified minimum number of hours for the service component. Although there were substantial differences across participants, respondents reported that they averaged 47.9% of class time for service-learning (range

0%–100%; SD = 33.8) and spent an average of 34.5 hours (range 0–499 hours; SD = 37.2) outside of class on the service-learning activity.

For the online (Hybrid I) tutoring course described previously, students (N = 50) in five semesters (Fall 2009 and Spring 2010 taught by me, and Fall 2011, Spring 2012, and Fall 2012 taught by another instructor) of this course participated in the surveys. These students were 90% female, 56% White, and predominantly seniors (48%), though 28% were at the master's level. The class was for variable credit (1–3 hours), and the amount of time reported by students spent on the service-learning component was 50% of course time (SD = 37.9) and 48.1 hours outside class (SD = 24.2).

Variables and Analyses

For this investigation, I created four composite variables to represent the student learning outcomes of interest. These were created from questionnaire items that used a 5-point Likert-type scale for responses (*strongly disagree* to *strongly agree*; higher scores reflected greater agreement with the prompts). The composite variables were created from related items reflecting commonly found student learning outcomes in the academic, personal, and civic domains (e.g., Eyler & Giles, 1999); specifically, improved *academic learning* of the course content (composed of three questionnaire items, which related to each other with a Cronbach's alpha (α) = .781), *critical thinking/moral reasoning* (seven items, α = .899), *personal/professional skills development* (six items, α = .858), and *commitment to service* (four items, α = .821).[5]

First Analysis: Contribution of Online Discussion to Learning Outcomes

Other items from the questionnaire were used as covariates to investigate the contribution of the online component to these learning outcomes. One prompt in the questionnaire asked students, "To what extent did your course emphasize the following: Online (e.g., eLC) discussion?" This was used to gauge the amount of online interaction involved in the course and offered five possible responses that were coded from 5 to 1: *very much, quite a bit, some, very little,* or *does not apply.* Student responses showed a range of online discussion: 16.8% reported *very much,* 12.2% reported *quite a bit,* 16.9% reported *some,* and about half reported *very little* (34.9%) or no (*does not apply,* 18.6%) online component.

Taking part in critical reflective writing, whether in class, online, or as homework, is a well-known service-learning practice with high impact (Eyler & Giles, 1999, p. 173). So, one concern was that any possible impact found from online discussion could be simply an artifact representing a greater amount of reflection overall in courses with online reflection rather than having anything to do with the online format per se. Because students also self-reported the amount of "journaling/reflective writing" in their service-learning course on the same scale as the online discussion item, I incorporated this variable into the analysis as a covariate to help isolate the unique contribution of the online component versus just "reflection" itself.

Likewise, online instruction and service-learning are suggested to foster improved relationships between faculty and students (Howard, 2001; Lewis & Abdul-Hamid, 2006). As such a relationship developed between student and teacher through the service-learning activity itself could conceivably lead to more intense student engagement within the online writing setting, I wanted to also take this into account in the analysis. In the end-of-course survey, students responded to the prompt, "My relationship with the course instructor or teaching assistant was more positive as a result of the service-learning activity" (5-point Likert scale); therefore, this was also used as a covariate.

For each of the four composite outcome variables of interest, I conducted a regression analysis; first, I incorporated variables for the *amount of overall reflective journaling* reported and the *relationship with the instructor* from the service activity; second, I added in the variable representing the *amount of online discussion*. The change in effect on the student learning outcome variable represented uniquely by the addition of online discussion is reflected in the change in the R-squared and F values, reported in Table 9.1. As Table 9.1 shows, for each outcome variable, the online component had a statistically significant influence beyond that provided by the frequency of reflective journaling and the relationship with the instructor.

However, the amount of influence that the online discussion uniquely contributed to the outcome variables is relatively small, as shown in the R-squared changes (varying between about 0.5% to 1.5% of the change in outcome variable scores). The standardized coefficients, shown in Table 9.2, indicate that in each instance the online discussion component has a smaller influence on the outcome variable than does either the level of reflective journaling or the student-instructor relationship.

Second Analysis: Comparing Hybrid I, Hybrid III, and Face-to-Face Service-Learning Courses

Next, I investigated differences in outcomes between three kinds of service-learning settings: Hybrid I, the single fully-online course, which I developed and taught, and that was subsequently taught by another instructor; Hybrid III eService-Learning, which blended face-to-face and online instruction; and standard face-to-face service-learning without significant online components.

TABLE 9.1

Regression of Reflective Journaling, Relationship With Instructor, and Online Discussion on Service-Learning Outcomes

Outcome Variable	Analysis	R-Squared	Std. Err. Est.	R-Squared Change	F Change	df1	df2	Sig. F Change
Academic learning	1	.304	.61	.304	390.5	2	1792	<.001*
	2	.309	.61	.005	14.1	1	1791	<.001*
Moral reasoning/ critical thinking	1	.264	.60	.264	320.2	2	1788	<.001*
	2	.270	.60	.006	15.7	1	1787	<.001*
Personal/ professional skills development	1	.345	.55	.345	472.4	2	1792	<.001*
	2	.360	.54	.016	44.5	1	1791	<.001*
Commitment to service	1	.301	.55	.301	385.8	2	1792	<.001*
	2	.305	.54	.004	10.7	1	1791	.001*

Note. For each regression, Analysis 1 includes variables for the *amount of overall reflective journaling* reported and the *relationship with the instructor* from the service activity; Analysis 2 includes those same variables plus the *amount of online discussion* variable as well.

* *p* value statistically significant at the ≤.05 level

TABLE 9.2

Standardized Coefficients (Betas) for Covariates From Full Model

Outcome Variable	Reflective Journaling	Enhanced Relationship With Instructor	Online Discussion
Academic learning	.101	.512	.074
Moral reasoning/ critical thinking	.204	.415	.081
Personal/profes- sional skills devel- opment	.141	.527	.127
Commitment to service	.167	.477	.065

As described previously, this Hybrid I course, housed in the UGA College of Education, engaged students in after-school tutoring with English-learning children, and used the online platform (eLC) for hosting the readings, instructional videos, and content modules, assignments, and reflections. The second and third groups were operationalized from student responses to the questionnaire prompt, "To what extent did your course emphasize the following: Online (e.g., eLC) discussion?" Students who responded *very much, quite a bit,* or *some,* were considered to be in a Hybrid III setting. Finally, those responding *very little* or *does not apply* were considered to be in a standard face-to-face service-learning course.

For each of the outcome variables described previously, I compared the self-reported results from students in the fully-online Hybrid I eService-Learning course with those from students reporting use of online discussions and with those from the other face-to-face service-learning courses in the database, using ANOVA and *t*-tests (see Table 9.3 and Table 9.4). The overall analysis of variance (Table 9.3) found statistically significant differences across the three types of instruction for each of the outcomes investigated. Next, the individual *t*-tests contrasting each pair of instruction type (Table 9.4) found that students reporting Hybrid III eService-Learning instruction had significantly better outcomes in all four categories investigated than did those in face-to-face-only instruction. Additionally, students in the Hybrid I classes outperformed those in face-to-face settings for three variables: academic learning, moral reasoning/critical thinking, and commitment to service. Students in the fully-online instruction (Hybrid I) also slightly outperformed the

TABLE 9.3
Descriptives (Mean, *SD*, *n*) and ANOVA Comparing Outcomes by Course Type

Outcome Variable	Hybrid I	Hybrid III	Face-to-Face	F (df)	p
Academic learning	Mean = 4.41 (.57) n = 49	Mean = 4.24 (.67) n = 859	Mean = 4.07 (.77) n = 1,007	15.86 (2,1910)	<.001*
Moral reasoning/ critical thinking	Mean = 4.40 (.54) n = 49	Mean = 4.21 (.66) n = 857	Mean = 4.05 (.73) n = 1,006	15.80 (2,1909)	<.001*
Personal/professional skills development	Mean = 4.06 (.67) n = 49	Mean = 4.20 (.64) n = 859	Mean = 3.97 (.70) n = 1,009	25.92 (2,1914)	<.001*
Commitment to service	Mean = 4.61 (.45) n = 49	Mean = 4.47 (.58) n = 858	Mean = 4.33 (.71) n = 1,006	12.79 (2,1910)	<.001*

Note. *p value statistically significant at the ≤ .05 level.

TABLE 9.4
***t*-Tests and Effect Sizes Comparing Outcomes Between Instruction Types**

Outcome Variable	Hybrid I Versus Hybrid III	Hybrid I Versus Face-to-Face	Hybrid III Versus Face-to-Face
Academic learning	t = 1.73, p = .083 Cohen's d = 0.115	t = 3.04, p = .002* Cohen's d = 0.187	t = 5.08†, p < .001* Cohen's d = 0.235
Moral reasoning/ critical thinking	t = 1.99, p = .047* Cohen's d = 0.132	t = 3.30, p = .001* Cohen's d = 0.203	t = 4.88, p < .001* Cohen's d = 0.226
Personal/professional skills development	t = 1.47, p = .142 Cohen's d = 0.098	t = 0.84, p = .40 Cohen's d = 0.052	t = 7.20, p < .001* Cohen's d = 0.333
Commitment to service	t = 2.04†, p = .046* Cohen's d = 0.265	t = 4.01†, p < .001* Cohen's d = 0.461	t = 4.57†, p < .001* Cohen's d = 0.211

Note. † Equal variances not assumed. *p value statistically significant at the ≤ .05 level.

Hybrid III students on moral reasoning/critical thinking and on commitment to service, but were statistically equivalent for academic learning outcomes and personal/professional skills development. The effect sizes (Cohen's *d*), also reported in Table 9.4 for each contrast, tended to be small.

Discussion

Students who reported that their service-learning course work incorporated online discussion (Hybrid III eService-Learning) also reported higher levels of learning outcomes from the service-learning experience, across all the variables investigated. Likewise, for most of these outcomes, students in the Hybrid I course whose instruction was offered fully online also reported greater learning outcomes than face-to-face instruction, and, in two areas, slightly better outcomes than the Hybrid III setting. There was no evidence that students in eService-Learning courses underperformed compared to the face-to-face instructional settings. Likewise, the regression analyses found that the inclusion of the online discussion component across the whole data set of courses had a small but statistically significant influence on learning outcomes, above and beyond the contribution of overall reflection activities and the student-instructor relationship. Does that suggest, then, that all instructors should begin requiring more online discussion in their service-learning courses?

Several caveats are important here. Waldner et al. (2012) cautioned sensitivity to the structural differences revealed in their typology and their potential for resulting in "radically different service or course learning outcomes" (p. 138). Clearly, we would expect that the quality and structure of the online discussions could influence student outcomes. However, the end-of-course surveys used here do not provide specifics of how the online instructional components were (or were not) used by instructors and students. Without additional data on the actual ways in which the online discussions were structured (e.g., frequency, quantity, quality, type) and related both to other online content and activities and to the service components of the courses, it is difficult to definitively explain any causes for the reported student outcomes.

Are reported differences, for instance, reflecting structural features of the online course setting, or just individual student preferences and behaviors? Just as students in the same course may report spending varying amounts of time on the service activity, within a given course there may be a lot of variability among students in terms of how much online participation they accomplish. Assuming that the instructor's behaviors and course requirements for participation are the same for all students within a given course, varied outcomes might point to individual student differences in online participation preferences, expectations and activity rather than the course structure itself, which would suggest that the impacts of the frequency of online activity are not really under the instructor's control. Indeed, responses from the 50 students in the fully online instruction tutoring courses seem to bear this out; while most agreed that their course used *very much* (46%) or *quite a bit* (24%) of online discussion, 24% indicated it only used *some*, and a few participants (4%) marked *very little* or *does not apply* (2%).[6] Differences in the amount of student participation in online activities and in their affiliated learning outcomes could likewise conceivably both be artifacts of differing levels of student overall engagement; if a student is highly motivated to take part in the course, for instance, we might expect that both the amount of time they spend online and the quality of their learning outcomes could be greater than for a disengaged student. However, the data available for the current study do not allow for this level of disambiguation.

In the investigation into differences between Hybrid I and Hybrid III instruction, while one difference from the other eService-Learning courses in the sample was the fully online instructional component of the Hybrid I classes, it is also possible that observed differences in students' reported outcomes may be due to other factors (e.g., amount of time spent on-site, kind of service activity, etc.) not fully investigated here. For instance, it seems plausible that forming close relationships with children at the tutoring sites might be a more important mediating variable for students' willingness to continue to serve after the course, than the online format; likewise, no advantage was found for the Hybrid I course in terms of students' reported skills development outcomes. Again, rather than necessarily representing a difference in instructional type, this finding could simply be an artifact of the Hybrid I class being a nonrequired course open to students in any major; and, except for those planning a career in education, tutoring program activities may not be directly relevant to building students' professional skills.

Additionally, as the instrument used here was a voluntary, post hoc self-report questionnaire, it relies on students' self-reported responses, which may be susceptible to bias or inconsistent/incorrect recall or interpretation of course activities. Only about half of the eligible students in these courses completed questionnaires; without comparison data, it is impossible to confirm whether they are representative of the classes as a whole. Although these data represent a wide range of courses across several semesters, they do not represent all service-learning courses available and are from a single university setting, and as such may not be readily generalizable.

As shown, the unique contribution of the online discussion component to the variation in student learning outcomes is statistically significant in a positive direction, per the regression analyses. However, it is practically quite small, representing only a minor influence on those outcomes; the variation in the amount of online discussion experienced by a student explains only about 1% of the difference in student learning outcomes investigated here. Similarly, for the comparisons across instruction type, the effect sizes for the statistically significant differences across groups were consistently small (about 0.2). So, these results suggest that an instructor would still make a bigger impact through focusing on their relationship with the students through the service activity and through inclusion of critical reflection in any modality, rather than to restructure the course only for this possible benefit.

Conclusion

Thus, this multisemester, multicourse analysis of eService-Learning at the University of Georgia found student learning outcomes to be positively influenced in statistically significant ways (though with small overall effect size) by the amount of online discussion components reported by the participating students. Given that incorporating online components into service-learning can be challenging for instructors and students alike, this chapter affirms the value of eService-Learning.

Instructors seeking to gain entrée into eService-Learning might, therefore, productively "start small" through using online tools for discussion and reflection components in otherwise face-to-face courses and service activities. As addressed earlier, the online component in and of itself is not the most important predictor of quality, so, as with any service-learning class, attention should be paid to ensuring that eService-Learning also incorporates clear learning outcomes, quality of service placement, effective and critical reflection activities, and so on (see Eyler & Giles, 1999). This chapter's findings also suggest that, even within the same course, the amount of online activity seems to vary considerably from student to student, which suggests that instructors should also be attentive to student differences in online participation (qualitatively as well as quantitatively) and should structure their courses to be supportive of students at differing levels of comfort and access.

Future research could productively confirm, extend, and further clarify this chapter's work. For instance, analyses that hold constant factors such as the amount of time spent on the service activity, the kinds of service undertaken, and/or student demographics, might help ascertain how robust the unique impact of eService-Learning is on student outcomes. Clarifying the quantity and types of online activity—perhaps through comparing data not only from the student but also from the course instructor's perspective, and even the course catalog or syllabus—as well as gaining further insight into student engagement and motivation, would help determine if the reported benefits accrue due to the course structure and what the instructor does or from student motivational characteristics and behavior. However, even within the limits of the current investigation, it seems that there is clear value to be found in the implementation of eService-Learning. Online instruction and discussion can support the positive academic, social, and personal learning outcomes valued in service-learning, which should give credence to the goals of expanding, promoting, and investing in eService-Learning.

Notes

1. For more on the Office of Service-Learning and institutional information, see www.servicelearning .uga.edu and www.uga.edu

2. This is congruent with Waldner et al.'s (2012) overview of the literature they reviewed, inasmuch as most examples they found "already incorporated reflection virtually through discussion board postings, blogs, or journals" (p. 143).

3. See http://servicelearning.uga.edu/sl-course-survey/ for more on the survey.

4. All participation was approved by the university's institutional review board for human subjects research.

5. Cronbach's alpha scores of .70 or higher are generally considered an acceptable indicator of internal consistency. The original items used for each variable of interest are given in the appendix.

6. This also suggests that the use of students' self-reported amount of online discussion may not be the best proxy for whether a course should be considered eService-Learning or its typology.

References

Bailey, C. J., & Card, K. A. (2009). Effective pedagogical practices for online teaching: Perception of experienced instructors. *Internet and Higher Education, 12,* (3–4), 152–155.

Bennett, G., & Green, F. P. (2001). Promoting service learning via online instruction. *College Student Journal, 35*(4), 491–497. Retrieved from http://findarticles .com/p/articles/mi_m0FCR/is_4_35/ai_84017184/

Dailey-Hebert, A., Donnelli-Sallee, E., & DiPadova-Stocks, L. N. (Eds.). (2008). *Service eLearning: Educating for citizenship.* Charlotte, NC: Information Age.

Eyler, J., & Giles, D. E., Jr. (1999). *Where's the learning in service-learning?* San Francisco, CA: Jossey-Bass.

Gelmon, S. B., Holland, B. A., Driscoll, A., Spring, A., & Kerrigan, S. (2001). *Assessing service-learning and civic engagement: Principles and techniques.* Providence, RI: Campus Compact.

Howard, J. (2001, Summer). Service-learning course design workbook [Companion volume]. *Michigan Journal of Community Service Learning.*

Kenworthy-U'Ren, A. (2008). Creating paths forward for service-eLearning: A ten-year review of the *Michigan Journal of Community Service Learning.* In A. Dailey-Hebert, E. Donnelli-Sallee, & L. N. DiPadova-Stocks (Eds.), *Service eLearning: Educating for citizenship* (pp. 9–22). Charlotte, NC: IAP.

Lewis, C. C., & Abdul-Hamid, H. (2006). Implementing effective online teaching practices: Voices of exemplary faculty. *Innovative Higher Education, 31*(2), 83–98.

Matthews, P. H. (2011). Online education and service-learning. In S. Clouser & C. Clark (Eds.), *Teaching with technology volume 2: The stories continue.* Learning Technology Consortium. Retrieved from http://ltcessays.files.wordpress.com/2011/04/05-matthews-service.pdf

Matthews, P. H. (2012, September). *Knowing and doing, connected via technology: Influence of online service-learning on student outcomes.* Paper presented at the annual meeting of the International Association for Research on Service-Learning and Community Engagement, Baltimore, MD.

Post, S. W. (2008). Service-eLearning: A burgeoning field. In A. Dailey-Hebert, E. Donnelli-Sallee, & L. N. DiPadova-Stocks (Eds.), *Service eLearning: Educating for citizenship* (pp. 23–28). Charlotte, NC: IAP.

Toncar, M., Reid, J., Burns, D., Anderson, C., & Nguyen, H. (2006). Uniform assessment of the benefits of service learning: The development, evaluation, and implementation of the scale. *Journal of Marketing Theory and Practice, 41*(3), 223–238.

Waldner, L. S., McGorry, S. Y., & Widener, M. C. (2012). E-service-learning: The evolution of service-learning to engage a growing online student population. *Journal of Higher Education Outreach and Engagement, 16*(2), 123–150.

APPENDIX
Survey Items Used for Composite Variables

Composite Variable	Survey Items
Academic learning	• The service-learning project in this course helped me see how the material covered can be useful in everyday life or other situations. • The service-learning project in this course helped me better understand the subject matter. • Ideas or concepts from other courses were useful to the service-learning component of this course.
Critical thinking/ moral reasoning	• The service-learning project in this course helped me better understand people of different ages, abilities, cultures, and/or economic backgrounds. • The service-learning project in this course encouraged me to seek additional opportunities to learn about people of different ages, abilities, cultures, and/or economic backgrounds. • The service-learning project in this course made me aware of some of my own biases and prejudices. • The service-learning project in this course helped me clarify my personal values. • The service-learning project in this course required me to make judgments about how to behave in new social settings. • The service-learning project in this course made me more aware of my possible impact on others. • The service-learning project in this course helped me reconsider some of my former attitudes about social problems.
Personal/professional skills development	• Through the service-learning project in this course, I enhanced my ability to manage my time efficiently. • Through the service-learning project in this course, I enhanced my ability to plan a project. • Through the service-learning project in this course, I enhanced my ability to review my work and evaluate my success at attaining my goals. • Through the service-learning project in this course, I enhanced my ability to work as a member of a team. • Through this course, I developed a greater sense of personal responsibility for my own learning. • The knowledge I gained in this course has made me more marketable in my chosen profession.

(Continues)

Composite Variable	*Survey Items*
Commitment to service	• After this course is over I will probably volunteer or participate in some way with the community or individuals served by this course. • Service-learning courses like this one can provide real benefits to people in the community. • The work I did in this course benefited some segment of the community. • I would be interested in participating in other courses with a service-learning component.

PART THREE

NEXT STEPS AND FUTURE DIRECTIONS

10

COMMUNITY ENGAGEMENT AND TECHNOLOGY FOR A MORE RELEVANT HIGHER EDUCATION

John Hamerlinck

In my years of being in the business of promoting community engagement in higher education, I have seen the proponents of community-centered education on college and university campuses continually struggle in an attempt to "institutionalize" civic engagement on their campuses from their positions on the institution's periphery. Although they have been tilting at the windmill of higher education's deeply rooted, sometimes archaic and seemingly impenetrable cloak of tradition just to get a little more respect, societal change, especially change driven by information technology, has emerged with promising opportunities to move their work from the margins to the core of higher education's mission.

I suggest that we quit asking for polite recognition and acknowledgment and that instead we boldly claim that community-engaged educational strategies, like community-based participatory research and problem-based service-learning, together with mobile and social 21st-century technologies and student dispositions, are in fact at the forefront of where higher education needs to go. We should embrace and demonstrate our ability to deliver a more connected, personal, creative, open, and relevant educational experience.

Rather than lay out a detailed road map, I hope to offer a case for support of the idea that the time is right for community engagement, hand in hand with popular technologies, to provide a relevant model of higher education delivery in today's world. Let's start by considering why higher education might be ready to benefit from disruptive change.

Troubling Times in Higher Education

There are an increasing number of people suggesting that higher education is the next industry bubble to burst. A number of factors are contributing to the idea that it needs some transformative change sooner rather than later. Here are just three:

- *Cost:* Even though the data suggesting that college graduates make more money over their lifetimes still hold true, the fact is that the cost of attending college is out of control. Since 1985, the overall consumer price index has risen 115%, while the college education inflation rate has risen nearly 500% (Odland, 2012).
- *Student success:* The average 6-year graduation rate at 4-year institutions across the country is 55.5% (National Center for Higher Education Management Systems, 2013). Yes, measuring graduation rates is more complex than it seems on the surface, but in an era when there are calls for more and more people than ever to attend college, it seems like we should warn new students that a large percentage of them won't get the credential they are investing in.
- *Debt:* Whether you graduate or not, you are probably going to owe lots of money when you leave college. Student loan debt has topped one trillion dollars in the United States. Two thirds of the class of 2011 held student loans upon graduation, and the average borrower owed $26,600 (Ellius, 2012). To put one trillion dollars into perspective, let's say that you have a job that pays you $40,000 per year. It would take you 25 million years to earn a trillion dollars.

These realities have led to increased public scrutiny of how higher education conducts its business. There is also a looming financial crisis within many institutions. A number of campuses appear to be in danger of financial demise. According to a recent study from Bain & Company, almost one third of colleges and universities in the United States are in "real financial trouble" (Denneen & Dretler, 2012). These institutions have financial statements that are significantly weaker than they were just a few years ago. Simply put, these institutions "have more liabilities, higher debt service and increasing expense without the revenue or the cash reserves to back them up" (Denneen & Dretler, 2012).

Some of the most innovative thinking about learning and about the emerging roles for higher education is coming out of places many civic engagement advocates are not currently looking. Education technologists and learning theorists outside of the usual civic engagement canon have presented some useful frameworks. David Wiley is the kind of thinker whose work can help us think about a vision for community engagement. Wiley is currently on leave from Brigham Young University and leading Lumen Learning, an organization dedicated to supporting and improving the adoption of open educational resources by middle schools, high schools, community and state colleges, and universities (Wiley, Green, & Soars, 2012). One could contend that Wiley's work is about community engagement at its core. In 2007, he taught a course at his institution and invited the rest of the world to participate. The syllabus and readings were all freely available online. All student writing was done online as well. According to Wiley, "The result was a group of approximately 60 people from around the world who read, worked, wrote, and discussed together—and fewer than 10 of them were registered for credit at my university" (Young & Wiley, 2009). To Wiley, the nonregistered community participants were not a burden to his university's resources but rather performed a public service by enhancing the education of the registered students.

Wiley also reminded us of how slow higher education is to change, despite a rapidly changing world:

> About 500 years ago, the primary mode of teaching in the university was to come in with blank sheets of paper and listen to the professor recite from a manuscript so you could make your own copy of the book. There was an opportunity 500 years ago with the invention of the press to radically change education. But that didn't happen. The lecture is still the primary model. Now we have the birth of the Internet. If we only get these opportunities twice a millennium, we should try to use them. (Kamenetz, 2013, p. 110)

Higher education's reluctance to embrace change was also expressed by Cathy Davidson of Duke University, author of 20 books, most recently *Now You See It: How the Brain Science of Attention Will Transform the Way We Live, Work and Learn*:

> Virtually every feature of traditional formal education was created between 1850 and 1919 to support the Industrial Age. . . . We're stuck with Henry Ford's assembly line from kindergarten through grad school! But our world

has changed! With the Internet we don't need the same kind of hierarchical structures. (Kamenetz, 2013)

A community-engaged education, one that involves active, collaborative, and student-directed learning, is a key to making higher education relevant to more students. The same kind of learning described by Harvard professor Eric Mazur in his 1997 book *Peer Instruction* transforms classrooms because it more closely resembles how we learn things outside of a classroom on a daily basis. We discuss things with friends and colleagues, generate new questions, and weigh options based on the information available. If you consider that this is exactly what social media has enabled people to do in terms of sharing and collaborating, it is clear that YouTube, Twitter, and the rest are also informing learning on a daily basis.

To some extent, information technology has nudged bits and pieces of higher education into the 21st century. What we need, however, is more than simply finding faster or more efficient ways to do things within the confines of traditional notions of college teaching and learning. People who have had portable, digital technology available to them their whole life find less relevance in memorizing notes and taking tests. They literally have a world at their fingertips with a diverse collection of wisdom at their disposal, as well as a diverse set of real problems to solve. The real opportunities to put significance and consequence into education emerge when an already existing networked view of the world can be viewed through a community lens.

Community-Engaged Teaching

> Strangely enough, digital technologies are forcing us to recognize the power of the collective and social. (Bollier, 2008)

There is a belief by some people that the Internet and online activity are isolating and, in fact, have the opposite effect that community-engaged learning like community-based participatory research and service-learning is trying to achieve. The adoption of technologies has always been accompanied by people warning about what we will lose as the result of innovations. I have no desire to dive into that history here. A considerable amount of recent research, however, has suggested that there is little to fear. According to research by the Pew Internet and American Life Project, the Internet and mobile phones are not linked to social isolation. In fact, online activity can even lead to larger, more diverse social networks (Hampton, Sessions, Her, & Rainie, 2009).

You are familiar with the *digital divide*, the access gap to technology that limits low-income people's access to the world through technology. Wiley and Hilton (2009) suggested that there is also a *daily divide*: "Individuals with abundant access to information and communication technologies who have habits of effective use of these technologies in information-seeking and problem-solving activities are unable to make effective use of these technologies in typical higher education settings."

As we send students out into the community to serve and to do research, we too often forget that they are carrying around in their pockets an extraordinary amount of computing power and access to the most advanced communications networks in the world. Why wouldn't we want them to use those tools in support of their service to the community?

Through my work at Minnesota Campus Compact's Center for Digital Civic Engagement, I have tried to identify portable, digital technologies that could complement all types of civic engagement in higher education. Here are some examples in just three categories.

Mapping: With mapping tools like the Google Maps, any number of social mapping projects are possible. SeeClickFix (http://seeclickfix.com) and City Sourced (www.citysourced.com) are two examples of sites that use mapping to engage citizens in identifying public safety and infrastructure issues in a community. Residents report potholes, vandalism, blocked bike lanes, and so on via their phone or computer. The information goes directly to a news site, and alerts are sent to city officials. There are also opportunities through mapping to support communities of interest. For example, the transgender community was involved in the development of http://safe2pee. org, a site that maps locations of public restrooms across the country that have gender-free bathrooms or traditionally gendered single stall or locking bathrooms. Hundreds of examples of maps for hundreds of purposes can be found on the Google Maps Mania blog (http://googlemapsmania.blogspot. com).

Data collection: Spreadsheets and other documents can be accessed via mobile devices in Google Drive (formerly Google Docs). Services like Rapid SMS (http://rapidsms.org) have a text message framework that manages data collection using basic mobile phones, presenting information on the Internet as soon as it is received. It is not constrained to any particular kind of mobile device, and you don't need to install any software on your phone to use it. If you are doing remote fieldwork or international work, FrontlineSMS turns a laptop and a mobile phone into a central communications hub. Once installed, the program enables users to send and receive text messages with groups of people through mobile phones. Of course, you could also do a version of the same thing through Twitter.

Dissemination: Sites like Themeefy (http://themeefy.com) and Scoop.it (www.scoop.it) can be used to create online magazines around a community or an issue. If you are interested in sharing audio interviews and reporting online, you can use sites like AudioBoo (http://audioboo.fm) and ipadio (www.ipadio.com). When you use social media services like Facebook, YouTube, Twitter, and so on, you can use Storify (www.storify.com) to tell stories using social media such as tweets, photos, and videos. You can search multiple social networks from one place and then drag individual elements into your story.

These examples just barely scratch the surface of the possibilities to support civic engagement with freely available technologies that students are already poised to use. We should not let higher education's daily divide extend to our community work.

21st-Century Technology

Over the past couple of decades, technology has changed how we do almost everything. It has changed how we work (telecommuting, webinars), how we learn (online search, data mapping, digital libraries), how we play (booking travel, online auctions), how we do business (e-commerce, marketing, banking), how we communicate (mobile phones, texting, tweets), and a list of other aspects of our life too long to mention. We are not simply using Internet-based tools to do things; we are thinking in new ways. For example, when I run into a computer problem—let's say some sort of Windows annoyance—I don't have to necessarily contact some technical support person. I simply type an error message or a brief description of my problem in a search engine and find that someone else has already had and solved that problem and is willing to share the solution with me. Many answers to questions previously residing only with "experts" are now available through an open gift economy of sorts. In 2012, the Encyclopedia Britannica stopped its presses after 244 years of publication. Wikipedia made the old model obsolete. As Clay Shirky (2010b) noted, "Wikipedia took the idea of peer review and applied it to volunteers on a global scale, becoming the most important English reference work in less than 10 years. Yet the cumulative time devoted to creating Wikipedia, something like 100 million hours of human thought, is expended by Americans every weekend, just watching ads."

The Evolution of Education Through Technology and Community Engagement

In Table 10.1, Wiley and Hilton (2009) offered two useful side-by-side comparisons illustrating ways that education has failed to adjust to a portable, digital world. This failure is not about technology adoption. It is about the

TABLE 10.1

David Wiley: Then Versus Now, Education Versus Everyday

Then	*Versus*	*Now*		*Education*	*Versus*	*Everyday*
Analog	=>	Digital		Analog	=>	Digital
Tethered	=>	Mobile		Tethered	=>	Mobile
Isolated	=>	Connected		Isolated	=>	Connected
Generic	=>	Personal		Generic	=>	Personal
Consumption	=>	Creating		Consumption	=>	Creating
Closed	=>	Open		Closed	=>	Open

Note. Adapted from Wiley and Hilton (2009).

inability of educators to effectively respond to societal changes in communication and knowledge acquisition that have been made possible because of information and communications technologies.

If we replace the word *everyday* with the word *community*, we can begin to recognize the benefits of social media and other technologies that augment the reality of our everyday lives. The *education versus everyday* comparison, in particular the last four concepts—connected, personal, creating, and open—might also create a set of goals for anyone seeking to make education more relevant. Let us briefly explore each of these areas and begin to see how community engagement complements efforts to achieve these goals for higher education.

Higher education has made strides in going both digital and mobile. It is in the areas of making education more connected, personal, creative, and open, however, that an approach utilizing appropriate technologies and community engagement can help make education more relevant to today's students. These four areas can all be enhanced through civic engagement and through technologies which students are already embracing.

Connected

People who use the Internet every day are constantly engaged in connected learning. Tapping the wisdom that exists in the community is a hallmark of community-engaged education. Creating opportunities for that wisdom to be shared digitally is at the center of the life of today's students. Connected learning is the difference between having a works cited page and having live links to people, information, and knowledge. This may come as a surprise, but not all of these links are from inside the academy.

Connectivism, a learning theory popularized by educational theorists like Stephen Downes and George Siemens, is the theory that knowledge and learning can be described and explained using network principles. It seeks to explain complex learning in a rapidly changing social digital world. This type of networked learning has a lot in common with pedagogies like service-learning. According to Downes, connectivist pedagogy creates an "authentic community of practice." He said, "To teach is to model and demonstrate—to learn is to practice and reflect" (Downes, 2007; 2013).

Connected teaching and learning is complemented by our ability to use various types of social media and to create and share information and knowledge. Table 10.2 reflects some work by Dr. Sarah Smith-Robbins (2008) from Indiana University. It points out that students can get many of the same things from higher education and social media. This suggests that a community, whether it is a geographical community or a community of interest, could be valuable in a learning environment.

This isn't to suggest that higher education does not add unique value. It is merely a reminder that a great deal of learning takes place outside of academia. I am 54 years old and have two college degrees. If I were to estimate the percentage of everything that I know that I learned in college, it would be maybe one one-millionth of one percent. Everything else has been learned through my life experience, in various sectors and aspects of community life and personal curiosity.

TABLE 10.2
Sarah Smith-Robbins: Higher Education and Social Media

Valued Characteristic	*Higher Education*	*Social Media*
Membership in intellectual and social affinity groups	X	X
Access to resources and experts	X	X
Engaging in intellectual discussions	X	X
Accumulate and develop skills for employment	X	X
Association with professional community	X	X
Establish social and professional network	X	X
Enhance personal and professional reputation	X	X
Share enthusiasm for common interests	X	X
Build skills	X	X

Note. Adapted from Robbins (2008).

People construct meaning for a new idea by relating it to ideas or processes they already understand. Most of that understanding comes from outside of the classroom. David Weinberger, perhaps best known as a coauthor of the *Cluetrain Manifesto* (Levine, Locke, Searls, & Weinberger, 2000) reminded us that "knowledge isn't in our heads; it's between us . . . social knowing is never finished" (Weinberger, 2007, p. 147). The connectedness that exists in communities extends into the social media world. Learning that takes place in site-based service-learning, for example, does not have to end there. If I serve at an organization and develop a relationship with people there, I am not just an asset they had for a short period of time. Similarly, I do not stop learning from that experience because I continue to have the relationship.

Personal

How did you learn things 20 years ago? How do you learn things now? If you agree that most of what a person learns, they learn outside of traditional classroom learning environments, then it is important to realize that everyone has a personal learning network (PLN), the entire collection of people with whom you engage and exchange information, usually online. In the pre-Internet days your PLN included the "street smarts" gained from experience, television, radio, and whatever books, magazines and newspapers you read. Today, your PLN also includes social media, networks of friends, acquaintances and people with common interests from around the world. Your PLN allows you to crowdsource solutions to problems. Crowdsourcing presents a problem to a community, asks the community for solutions, lets the community scrutinize the suggested solutions, and then invites them to help implement the solutions. Many online tools support crowdsourcing. They include: All Our Ideas (www.allourideas.org), IdeaScale (http://ideascale.com), Google Moderator (www.google.com/moderator), and Crowdmap (http://crowdmap.com).

According to EDUCAUSE, a nonprofit association of information technology leaders and professionals committed to advancing higher education, the personal learning environment is "likely to become a fixture in educational theory, engendering widespread acknowledgment of its value, both of its framework and of its components. Scholars might find it important to maintain web updates on their own scholarship as new findings are posted elsewhere. Students will find themselves increasingly working collaboratively and relying on their network of contacts for information. As a result, students will probably more quickly develop the skill to sort the authoritative from the noise" (EDUCAUSE, 2013).

Another phenomenon at the intersection of higher education and information technology and personalization is the extraordinary emergence of online college courses. Whether synchronous, asynchronous, blended, flipped, massive open online courses (MOOCs), or some other hybrid, it is clear that online learning is a significant and important part of higher education. The 2012 Survey of Online Learning conducted by the Babson Survey Research Group gives us an idea of just how important online courses are to higher education. Key report findings include the following:

- Over 6.7 million students were taking at least one online course during the Fall 2011 term, an increase of 570,000 students over the previous year.
- Thirty-two percent of higher education students now take at least one course online.
- Seventy-seven percent of academic leaders rate the learning outcomes in online education as the same or superior to those in face-to-face classes.
- The proportion of chief academic leaders who say online learning is critical to their long-term strategy is at a new high of 69.1% (Allen & Seaman, 2013).

The desire for greater personalization of the educational experience has played no small part in the emergence of online learning. It is not just the convenience of taking courses on one's own schedule that appeals to students. Personalization also comes from the increasing number of open education options (more on that in a bit).

So what does all of this talk about online learning have to do with community engagement? Too many of higher education's civic engagement proponents have ignored online learning despite its being the fastest growing area of higher education. They do so at their own peril, because better understanding how to merge these two things creates tremendous opportunity.

Consider one of the greatest benefits of a pedagogy like service-learning: the development of those core, transferable work habits, competences, and dispositions traditionally known as "soft skills." Educational experiences such as community-based participatory research or service-learning do much more than help students apply theory. They are also great ways for students to learn a variety of communication skills, as well as things like adaptability and conflict resolution. Those of us who are proponents of these pedagogies but who do not figure out how to effectively use them in online courses are denying increasing numbers of students an opportunity to develop these skills.

Another tremendous opportunity can be seized when students taking service-learning courses from geographically dispersed locations provide valuable service to communities that are not physical hosts to campuses. Online students do not live online. They live in communities. Wherever those communities are, online students can serve them. This will not only positively influence students' education but also have the additional benefit of extending a college's regional or even international profile and impact.

Creating

My contention is that creativity now is as important in education as literacy, and we should treat it with the same status . . . and the result is that we are educating people out of their creative capacities (Sir Ken Robinson, 2006).

In 2010, when I started the Center for Digital Civic Engagement, I did so for two reasons. The first was to collect whatever information I could about how people were attempting to do service-learning in online courses. The second was to plant the seeds of creativity in the higher education civic engagement community. I try to introduce widely available, mostly free technologies that might be adapted for use in data gathering and for documenting, evaluating, organizing, and sustaining community-based teaching and learning.

Social media integrates technology, social interaction, and content, transforming people from content consumers into content producers. Isn't this also the goal of civic engagement? Don't we want people to become producers of democracy and not just passive observers? So-called web 2.0 technologies have transformed people from mere consumers of content into curators and producers of content. This is similar to one of the goals of civic engagement: to turn students from passive participants into active participants of democracy.

In his book *Cognitive Surplus: Creativity and Generosity in a Connected Age*, Shirky (2010a) provided numerous examples of how people with a common predisposition both to create and to share can connect through various web 2.0 technologies and leverage their online networks to affect change in communities around the world. His case studies demonstrate how people's natural desire to both create and share is making positive things happen every day. I have already mentioned the creation of Wikipedia. The following are two examples based on fans of musicians being connected to those celebrities online.

During an embargo of U.S. beef imports to Korea, a deal was in the works to remove the embargo. One tweet from a member of the popular Korean boy band DBSK expressed disapproval of lifting the embargo. Suddenly, thousands of young Korean girls were taking to the streets to protest the import of U.S. beef. Though it was not a highly organized protest, the Korean government took notice. Slightly more understandable is the example of members of the Josh Groban Fan Club realizing that they were much more effective fund-raisers and organizers than the staff of the singer's foundation.

Ultimately the fans' work went on to improve the effectiveness and impact of that foundation.

People look to higher education for innovation. Innovation requires creativity, and creativity is inspired by community. As Masaru Ibuka, cofounder of Sony, said, "Creativity comes from looking for the unexpected and stepping outside your own experience" (ThinkExist.com, 2013). Stepping outside your own experience is also what community-engaged education is all about. Educators should take advantage of all of the tools and talents being cultivated in the information technology sector to cocreate solutions to the challenges faced by local and global communities.

Open

The community engagement/technology connection that is getting the most attention is perhaps the worldwide movement toward open education. Open Education Week is an effort coordinated by Open Education Consortium (formerly Open Course Ware Consortium), an association of hundreds of institutions and organizations around the world that are committed to the ideals of open education. Its definition of *open education* says that it "incorporates free and open learning communities, educational networks, teaching and learning materials, open textbooks, open data, open scholarship, open source educational tools and on and on. Open Education gives people access to knowledge, provides platforms for sharing, enables innovation, and connects communities of learners and educators around the world" (Open Education Week, 2013).

Openness is inextricably linked to making education more personal. David Wiley argued, "Education is first and foremost an enterprise of sharing. In fact, sharing is the sole means by which education is effected. If a teacher is not sharing what he or she knows with students, there is no education happening. Those educators who share the most thoroughly with the greatest proportion of their students are the ones we deem most successful" (Wiley et al., 2012).

The connection between open education and community goes to the core of civic life. The concept of openness isn't just about getting things for free. Stephen Downes captured this idea in his book *Free Learning*:

> In one sense, "free learning" means, of course, "learning for free," which in turn may be thought of as "learning without charge" or fee or cost, and also, learning freely, according to one's own will and direction. In another sense, "free learning" may be thought of as an imperative, a command, to release learning from its existing shackles, from its role as a colonizer and commoditizer of people and societies, and to set it free as a common cultural

heritage, like a language, like a cuisine, like a musical tradition. . . . I think that our common heritage is too valuable to slice and dice and apportion off to the highest bidder, and I think that the right of each person not only to consume, but also to contribute to, that heritage is a right that ought not easily be surrendered. Who we are as individuals, as a society, as a species, rides on the outcome of this. (Downes, 2011, pp. 6, 8)

The diversity of ideas in education should reflect the diversity of the community. One tremendous benefit of a community-engaged education is students get the opportunity to interact with people who are not like them and to see them as citizens and residents, as opposed to seeing them as parts of abstract groups or as statistics. People's comfort with being in the middle of a diverse community of learners might, in part, begin to explain the popularity of MOOCs. Learners in MOOCs are not sitting in a giant virtual classroom. They are seeking out affinity groups of learners who want the same thing from a course that they do. MOOCs are also like communities in that much of their activity (connections, learning, sharing) happens organically, as opposed to being disseminated from an expert through highly regulated channels. Educational theorist George Siemans (2012) said, "It is important to realize that MOOCs are not (yet) an answer to any particular problem. They are an open and ongoing experiment. They are an attempt to play with models of teaching and learning that are in synch with the spirit of the Internet."

Seizing an Opportunity

If you are a proponent of higher education who engages learners with communities, you have never been better positioned to demonstrate your contributions to a reimagined model of higher education that promises to be more relevant to today's learners. To take full advantage of this opportunity, you need to allow yourself to think of information technology and the Internet not as isolating or antisocial evils but as bridges and lifelines that support and enhance civic engagement and our sense of community.

A 2011 study supported by the MacArthur Foundation and the Center for Information and Research on Civic Learning and Engagement, found that youth who pursue their interests on the Internet are more likely to be engaged in civic and political issues and to be exposed to diverse political viewpoints (Cohen & Kahne, 2011). Those youth are *connected* to people who are passionate about the same things they are. They are constantly adding to their *personal* learning networks, while *creating* and sharing their own knowledge with an entire world of *open* platforms of people thinking globally and acting locally. We should see that their educational experience does the same. If this is where we are finding active, motivated students, why isn't higher education in that same space?

If we wait for best practices and peer review to dictate how we begin to connect and create with students in personal and open spaces, it will be too late. Civic engagement advocates within higher education can seize this opportunity today and be at the forefront of a more relevant higher education.

References

Allen, I. E., & Seaman, J. (2013). *Changing course: Ten years of tracking online education in the United States.* Retrieved March 30, 2013, from http://sloanconsortium .org/publications/survey/changing_course_2012

Bollier, D. (2008). *The commons as a new sector of value-creation.* Amsterdam, the Netherlands: De Balie Centre for Culture and Politics. Retrieved from http:// bollier.org/commons-new-sector-value-creation

Cohen, C. J., & Kahne, J. (2011). *Participatory politics: New media and youth political action.* Oakland, CA: YPP Research Network. Retrieved April 10, 2013, from http://ypp.dmlcentral.net/sites/all/files/publications/YPP_Survey_Report_ FULL.pdf

Davidson, C. (2001). *Now You See It: How the Brain Science of Attention Will Transform the Way We Live, Work, and Learn.* New York, NY: Viking Press.

Denneen, J., & Dretler, T. (2012). *The financially sustainable university.* Retrieved March 30, 2013, from http://www.bain.com/Images/BAIN_BRIEF_The_ financially_sustainable_university.pdf

Downes, S. (2007). *What connectivism is.* Retrieved February 3, 2007, from http:// halfanhour.blogspot.de/2007/02/what-connectivism-is.html

Downes, S. (2011). *Free learning* (Version 1.01). Retrieved April 10, 2013, from http://www.downes.ca/me/mybooks.htm

Downes, S. (2013). *What connectivism is.* Retrieved March 30, 2013, from http:// halfanhour.blogspot.com/2007/02/what-connectivism-is.html

EDUCAUSE. (2013). *Seven things you should know about personal learning environments.* Retrieved March 30, 2013, from http://net.educause.edu/ir/library/pdf/ ELI7049.pdf

Ellius, B. (2013). *Average student loan debt nears $27,000. CNN.* Retrieved March 30, 2013, from http://money.cnn.com/2012/10/18/pf/college/student-loan-debt/ index.html

Hampton, K. N., Sessions, E. J., Her, E. J., & Rainie, L. (2009). *Social isolation and new technology.* Washington, DC: Pew Internet and American Life Project. Retrieved from http://www.pewinternet.org/Reports/2009/18--social-isolation- and-new-technology.aspx

Kamenetz, A. (2013). *Learning and the web.* Retrieved March 30, 2013, from http:// learningfreedomandtheweb.org/Mozilla_LFW.pdf

Levine, R., Locke, C., Searls, D., & Weinberger, D. (2000). *The cluetrain manifesto.* New York, NY: Basic Books.

Mazur, E. (1997). *Peer instruction: A user's manual.* Upper Saddle River, NJ: Prentice Hall.

National Center for Higher Education Management Systems. (2013). *Graduation rates.* Retrieved from http://www.higheredinfo.org/dbrowser/index.php?submeasure=27&year=2009&level=nation&mode=data&state=0

Odland, S. (2012). *College costs out of control.* Retrieved March 30, 2013, from http://www.forbes.com/sites/steveodland/2012/03/24/college-costs-are-soaring/

Open Education Week. (2013). *About open education.* Retrieved April 10, 2013, from http://2013.openeducationweek.org/about-open-education/

Robbins, S. (2008). *Social media and education: The conflict between technology and institutional education, and the future.* Presentation at EDUCAUSE. Retrieved March 30, 2013, from www.slideshare.net/intellagirl/educause08-social-media-and-education-presentation

Robinson, K. (2006). *Ken Robinson says schools kill creativity.* Retrieved March 30, 2013, from http://www.ted.com/talks/ken_robinson_says_schools_kill_creativity.html

Shirky, C. (2010a). *Cognitive surplus: Creativity and generosity in a connected age.* New York, NY: Penguin.

Shirky, C. (2010b, June 4). Does the Internet make you smarter? *Wall Street Journal.* Retrieved from http://online.wsj.com/article/SB10001424052748704025304575284973472694334.html

Siemens, G. (2012). *MOOCs for the win!* Retrieved April 10, 2013, from http://www.elearnspace.org/blog/2012/03/05/moocs-for-the-win/

ThinkExist.com. (2013). *Masaru Ibuka quotes.* Retrieved March 30, 2013, from http://en.thinkexist.cm/quotes/masaru_Ibuka/

Weinberger, D. (2007). *Everything is miscellaneous: The power of the new digital disorder.* New York, NY: Henry Holt.

Wiley, D., Green, C., & Soars, L. (2012). *Dramatically bringing down the cost of education with OER.* EDUCAUSE issue brief. Retrieved from https://www.americanprogress.org/issues/labor/news/2012/02/07/11167/dramatically-bringing-down-the-cost-of-education-with-oer/

Wiley, D., & Hilton, J. (2009). Openness, dynamic specialization and the disaggregated future of higher education. *International Review of Research in Open and Distance Learning, 10*(5). Retrieved March 30, 2013, from http://www.irrodl.org/index.php/irrodi/article/view/768/1414

Young, J., & Wiley, D. (2009, July 15). Open teaching multiplies the benefit but not the effort [Web blog post]. *The Chronicle of Higher Education.* Retrieved from https://chronicle.com/blogs/wiredcampus/david-wiley-open-teaching-multiplies-the-benefit-but-not-the-effort/7271

11

CONCLUSIONS, RECOMMENDATIONS, AND FINAL THOUGHTS

Jean Strait

Before We Log Off . . .

So now that we have investigated the essential components of eService-Learning, examined models of each of the hybrid areas, and discovered where higher education may want to place its priorities, where is eService-Learning headed? When I first started using eService-Learning in 2004, I had no idea what technologies would be available in 2014. Social media has exploded on the learning stage, and course platforms have eased with maturity. There was no thought about anything going open source and now just about anyone can create some learning experience via video or application.

We believe eService-Learning will have many future applications. As K–12 schools grow and more alternative programs become available, it makes sense that students will be using eService-Learning in multiple communities and with multiple partners. When these same students enter higher education institutions, they will want to use this as a learning format. Community organizations could offer businesses community engagement for their employees by using eService-Learning models in the workplace. Imagine being able to serve right in your office and get work credit for doing so. We also envision that eService-Learning could be an untapped vehicle for older people and people with disabilities who are not able to leave their homes.

Recently, I created a tutoring program where wheelchair-bound and other people with disabilities could tutor in local elementary schools. The success rate appears to be phenomenal. First-grade students are improving their reading and writing skills while their mentors are improving their social and emotional skills in the community. My participants are enthusiastic that they can make a difference for someone else. Several others would also like to mentor but physically can't leave their place of residence. Imagine the benefit for all students to have daily, consistent tutoring with someone who really wants to spend quality time with them. I see this as something like AmeriCorps or Seniorcorp, where people with disabilities could also serve their community. One of my current participants, Jennifer, has really been adopted by the entire school community and even has a staff name tag for use at school. She feels like for the first time in her life she has a job and looks forward to helping the children. What this program has done for her self-esteem and belief in her own abilities has really been amazing to watch. If the state or federal agencies could integrate some type of stipend or salary to this tutoring, then many people with disabilities would be greatly helped with additional funding to offset the cost of equipment and medicines. It would be a win-win all around.

What about people who may be a bit older and living alone? Generativity can set in, leaving people feeling like they don't have anything to contribute. These folks could also benefit from eService by having the opportunity to serve youth and community partners. Many community organizations don't have the resources to hire individuals to assist them with high-need programs, and this may be one way to fill that void.

Using eService-Learning may even help reduce the carbon footprint currently generated through transportation gases and the movement of goods and services. It gives new meaning to using "local" in a global society. eService-Learning also integrates 21st-century skills.

Perhaps even more important, eService-Learning enables people to stay connected to issues and communities they are passionate about and want to contribute to, and it gives them a way to do that *when* they want. Imagine a student who likes to work on projects and service during the early morning hours or very late at night. If that is an optimal time for students to work, why not provide them ways to serve when they are at their most productive? Don't we also want to maximize on the skill sets community members have to offer?

In Cathy N. Davidson's (2011) book *Now You See It: How the Brain Science of Attention Will Transform the Way We Live, Work, and Learn*, she described a future where learning is based on the completion of skill sets, much like earning a merit badge in scouting organizations. I think she has something very powerful here to consider. As technology continues to improve and our ability to find ways to use it increases, learning will not be confined to a standard program. Learners will have to learn, unlearn, and relearn new material multiple times throughout their lifetime. eService-Learning would be a great way to assess what learners can gain and provide to others who may need that same skill set. The major caution here is to start small. Trying to create an initial eService-Learning project that is too much to manage could keep teachers, students, or community partners from ever attempting it again. Technology can dazzle users every day. The question becomes, "Just because we have it, should we use it?" Time and practice will reveal the answer.

Research and evaluation play important roles in the future of eService-Learning, but we have yet to know to what extent. Certainly, more research is needed on each of the hybrid models presented in this book, and more dialogue needs to occur around the critical issues and elements of eService-Learning. To that end, we have created a website that will encourage those discussions through blogs, resource sharing, and webinars to help infuse eService-Learning practice as a daily pedagogical strategy. We encourage you to contact us, ask questions, and discuss everything we present here. My grandmother used to say the only way to make something better is to wear it in. We invite all of you to try eService-Learning and see if it fits for you.

Reference

Davidson, C. N. (2011). *Now you see it: How brain science of attention will transform the way we live, work, and listen.* New York, NY: Viking.

EDITORS AND CONTRIBUTORS

Editors

Jean Strait serves as a professor in the Teacher Education Department at Hamline University, where she brings 25 years of firsthand experience teaching reading, literacy, and educational psychology in higher education urban classrooms. She has also developed and led urban teacher programs with service-learning components at two- and four-year colleges throughout the Twin Cities. Most recently, Jean spent three years as the director for the Center for Excellence in Urban Teaching at Hamline University. Jean is the first female Native American tenured full professor at Hamline; quite impressive, as only .04 % of professors worldwide are Native American.

In 2011 she received the President's Award for Service-Learning Advocacy and the Anna Arnold Hedgeman Center's Outstanding Faculty Award for teaching cultural diversity. In 2012, she received the International Service-Learning in Teacher Education's Rahima Wade Award for Outstanding Contributions to Service-Learning in Teaching Education in the United States. Jean has been highly recognized for her program, Each One, Teach One (EOTO), a distance service-learning project partnering college students in Minnesota with struggling middle school students in New Orleans, Louisiana.

In addition to her teaching endeavors, Jean presents nationally in a variety of formats. She has authored four books and contributed to several books on service-learning, civic engagement, and urban education.

Katherine J. Nordyke has been characterized by students as a "walking public affairs mission." Katherine has served as the director of the Office of Citizenship and Service-Learning (CASL) at Missouri State University (MSU) since January 2012 and received the 2014 Board of Governors' Award for Excellence in Public Affairs. The award recognizes three faculty and three staff members each year who excel in carrying forward Missouri State's public affairs missions. She holds a bachelor's and master's degree in leadership from Fort Hays State University and is nearing completion of her doctorate in education–instructional leadership with a focus in civic engagement and service-learning.

As director of CASL, Katherine has increased experiential learning opportunities for students; more than 6,000 students have participated in service-learning during the past three years. She works to create new community partnerships and projects that will have sustainable effects in addressing community problems and social justice issues for years to come. In partnership with the University of Alabama, Katherine initiated the FocusFirst Vision Screen program, a free vision screening program for children, youth, adults, and seniors. Through her efforts and those of MSU service-learning nursing, premedicine, and preoptometry students, over 1,200 children and adults in low-income and disadvantaged areas received free vision screenings in 2014.

Contributors

John Hamerlinck is a writer, trainer, and consultant with experience in the private, government, nonprofit, and philanthropic sectors. He worked at Minnesota Campus Compact for a decade, serving as associate director from 2009 to 2014. His work is rooted in a passionate commitment to finding and effectively mobilizing hidden or underappreciated capacities of individuals, organizations, and communities. John's interest in information and communications technology led him to establish the Center for Digital Civic Engagement in 2010. John has published numerous articles and book chapters on a variety of topics from popular culture to entrepreneurship. He has facilitated trainings in asset-based community development for groups nationwide. In 2014, he coedited *Asset-Based Community Engagement in Higher Education*. He holds a bachelor of arts in American studies and a master of science in social responsibility from St. Cloud State University.

Paul H. Matthews is the assistant director of the Office of Service-Learning at the University of Georgia, where he helps support faculty members, students, and community partners in applying academic skills and knowledge to address community needs and enhance student learning. Paul has been on the faculty at the University of Georgia since 1994 in departments including Romance languages, language and literacy education, and the Center for Latino Achievement & Success in Education (CLASE) in the College of Education. He was part of the Office of Service-Learning's first cohort of

Service-Learning Fellows in 2006 and developed a course supporting tutors of English-learning children, which he eventually taught in face-to-face, blended, and fully online iterations. After serving three years as a faculty affiliate with the Office of Service-Learning as Senior Scholar for Faculty Development, he joined the office full-time as assistant director in July 2010. In that role, he helps coordinate faculty development, tracks institutional reporting of service-learning and community engagement, conducts research and evaluation, and coordinates service-learning initiatives and student programs. Recently offered courses have ranged from a graduate seminar on service-learning course design, to an undergraduate course on social entrepreneurship, to an online minicourse on service-learning in STEM disciplines for the National Science Foundation-funded Center for the Integration of Research, Teaching and Learning network. Paul holds a doctorate in language education and has published and presented on topics including service-learning tutoring, research and evaluation of service-learning, service-learning with high-ability English learners, online service-learning, and institutional inputs and outcomes in service-learning.

Sue McGorry is professor of business and chair of business administration and marketing at DeSales University. She teaches both undergraduate and graduate courses in marketing, research, and data mining. Prior to her appointment at DeSales, she held marketing positions with Chase Manhattan Bank and AT&T. Sue has been teaching online since 1996, developing online service-learning projects with organizations such as the American Red Cross, Valley Youth House, the Eastern Pennsylvania Down Syndrome Center, United Way, the Diocese of Allentown, and many other organizations. Her professional memberships include the American Marketing Association (faculty adviser to the Delaware State University Chapter), the Atlantic Marketing Association, Multimedia Educational Resource for Learning and Online Teaching (MERLOT), and the Marketing Science Institute. She has published articles in *Qualitative Market Research*, *The Internet and Higher Education*, *Journal of Nonporofit and Public Sector Marketing*, and *Journal of Online Learning and Teaching*. McGorry holds a master of business administration and a doctor of philosophy in marketing and applied research.

Pauline Mosley holds a bachelor of science in math and a bachelor of science in computer science from Mercy College and a master of science in information systems and a doctorate of professional studies in computing from Pace University. She embarked upon a teaching career in 1986, working as a top corporate trainer for Personal Computer Learning Centers of America, Inc. where she trained Fortune 500 members in a myriad of software applications.

She is the recipient of the Who's Who Among America's Teachers award and is a full professor of information technology in Seidenberg School of Computer Science and Information Systems at Pace University in Pleasantville, New York. She teaches primarily LEGO robotics, Internet and network security, web design, and service-learning courses. Pauline's research interests include cognitive models for learning robotics and web development. She has explored pedagogical methodologies that explore the relationships between service-learning and learning and its long-term impact on students. She is a member of the Institute of Electrical and Electronic Engineers (IEEE) and frequently serves on the program committee of national conferences in information technology. Journals in which her research has appeared include the *Journal of Computing Sciences in Colleges, Across The Disciplines,* and *Academic Exchange Quarterly.*

Jane Turk is the coordinator of high-impact learning practices in Hamline University's Center for Teaching and Learning and serves as the program director for the undergraduate Liberal Education as Practice (LEAP) requirement, which focuses on connecting the liberal arts to the world of work and community engagement through experiential learning. Before joining the Center for Teaching and Learning, she served as Hamline's coordinator of civic engagement and service-learning. Before coming to Hamline, she completed graduate work on the history and regulation of public and commercial broadcasting in the United States and taught courses in media history, media writing, communication studies, and media theory. She has held teaching positions at colleges and universities including Hunter College (CUNY), Marymount Manhattan College, Lake Forest College, DePaul University, and Normandale Community College. Jane holds master of philosophy and master of arts degrees in communications from Columbia University and a bachelor of arts degree in communication and media studies and humanities and cultural studies from Macalester College. She resides in St. Paul with her husband and daughter.

Leora Waldner is an assistant dean for the College of Arts & Sciences in Global Campus/eTROY, and also serves as an associate professor of political science with Troy University's Master of Public Administration program. She received her PhD in City and Regional Planning from the University of California, Berkeley. An early pioneer of eService-Learning, she was inspired to transition her service-learning endeavors online when she was recruited to teach online over a decade ago. Since then, she and her students have partnered with local government agencies and nonprofit organizations to produce best practices and policy analysis research on subjects ranging from drowning-related racial disparities to health equity issues. Her work focuses on transforming online learning through eAdvising, eService-Learning, and mentoring other online instructors to craft truly transformative courses. Her team-based research on eService-Learning and eAdvising has received extensive attention, with nearly 2,000 downloads since 2012. She is also the author of *From Subpar to RockStar: 12 Strategies for Excellence in Online Nutrition Education*, developed for the Nutrition Educators of Health Professionals. Her academic research focuses on land-use planning and municipal incorporation. Her professional background in environmental planning involves over a decade of experience working for government agencies and consulting firms on environmental planning topics such as urban forestry and wetlands protection.

AAC&U. *See* Association of American
    Colleges and Universities
academic learning, 144
activism, 11
ADA. *See* Americans With
    Disabilities Act
advocacy service-learning, 12
affective learning, 101
All Our ideas, 157
American Association of Community
    Colleges, 45, 74
    requirements, 50
American Heart Association, 47
American Life Project, 152
Americans With Disabilities Act
    (ADA), 32–33, 49
AmeriCorps, 165
animal shelters, 97
artifacts, 26
arts organizations, 97
Ash, S. L., 41
Association of American Colleges and
    Universities (AAC&U), 14
    on high-impact educational
        practices, 16
AudioBoo, 154
Avalon High School, 28
    Hybrid III eService-Learning in, 106

Babson Survey Research Group, 72
Bain & Company, 150
Bemidji State University, 28
Bennett, G., 27
Blackboard, 48–49, 60, 64, 76
    EOTO and, 110
    in Hybrid II eService-Learning,
        92, 94

blogs, 49
Brigham Young University, 151
Burton, F., 28
    on Extreme eService-Learning, 122

Campus Compact, 45
Canvas, 48–49
career skills, 29–30
    CASL and, 87
    in student interviews, 115
Carnegie Classification, 79
Carnegie Foundation, 131
CASL. *See* Citizenship and Service-
    Learning
cell phones, 110
Center for Digital Civic
    Engagement, 159
Center for Information and Research
    on Civic Learning and
    Engagement, 161
Chatware, 126
churches, 97
Citizenship and Service-Learning
    (CASL), 55, 71
    academic development, 87
    career and, 87
    civic responsibility and, 87
    communication, 87
    core assessment
        components, 84
    critical thinking, 87
    Dashboard, 84, 85
    Missouri State University, 82–85
    outcomes, 87–88
    Oversight Committee, 74, 82,
        83, 84
    sample dashboard, 85

Service-Learning Course
  Outcomes, 82
 teamwork and, 87
City Sourced, 153
civic based service-learning, 91
civic engagement
 defined, 7
 at Hamline University, 111–12
 in Hybrid II eService-Learning,
  99–100
 pedagogy and, 9–10
 revitalizing, 8–9
 teaching, 9–10
 wheel of, 10
civic knowledge, 8
civic learning
 cycle of, 8
 defined, 7–8
civic responsibility, 13
civic skills, 8
civic values, 8
Clayton, P. H., 41
client-based courses, 25
clients
 commitment from, 125–26
 initial meeting with, 125
 relationships, 127
Cluetrain Manifesto (Weinberger), 157
*Cognitive Surplus: Creativity and
  Generosity in a Connected Age*
  (Shirky), 61
collaboration, 13
commitment to service, 145
communication, 29
 CASL and, 87
 eService-Learning, 64
 in student interviews, 113, 115
 technology and, 64
community-based research, 91
 defined, 11
community engagement, 70, 149–50
 data collection and, 153
 dissemination, 153–54
 in Extreme eService-Learning, 128

mapping and, 153
 online, 60–61, 136
 pedagogies of, 11
 teaching and, 152–54
 transgender, 153
community partners
 in Extreme eService-Learning, 122
 in Hybrid II eService-Learning, 102
 profiles, 97
community service, 11
composite variables, 144–45
computers, 58–59
conduct, 54
Confidentiality, Conduct, and Liability
  Release form, 49
 sample, 54–55
connective learning, 100
 from eService-Learning, 101
connectivism, 155–57
consulting based service-learning, 91
content delivery, 63
Cornelius-White, Jef, 80
course content
 in Extreme eService-Learning,
  121–22
 in Hybrid II eService-Learning,
  95–96
 IS/IT curriculum, 95
 technology in, 76–77
course development
 client-based courses, 25
 eService-Learning, 46–51, 53
 Extreme eService-Learning, 123–24
 Hybrid II eService-Learning, 92
 online courses, 33–35, 42, 158, 161
 service-learning, 56, 75–76
 technology-based, 95–96
 transactional, 26
 transformational, 26
 web design, 93
Cravens, X., 83
creativity, 159–60
critical thinking, 144
Crowdmap, 157

A Crucible Moment: College Learning and Democracy's Future, 8
cultural competence, 70

Dailey-Herbert, Amber, 41
daily divide, 155
data collection
    community engagement and, 153
    Missouri State University and, 79–80
    technology for, 64–65
Davidson, Cathy, 151–52, 165–66
day care centers, 97
deliberative dialog, 11
demographics, 79–80
Depot House, 108
DFW. *See* Drop, Fail, Withdraw
digital divide, 152–53
digital immigrants, 61
DiPadova-Stocks, Laurie N., 41
direct service-learning, 11
dissemination, 153–54
Distinguished Visiting Scholar, 36
Distributed Learning in Teacher
    Education (DLiTE), 28
Donnelli-Sallee, Emily, 41
Downes, Stephen, 156, 160–61
Down syndrome advocacy, 27
Dreamweaver, 91
Drop, Fail, Withdraw (DFW), 84
Duke University, 151–52

Each One, Teach One (EOTO), 28,
    60, 106
    Blackboard and, 110
    civic awareness and, 111
    model, 109
    program goals, 109
    student academic achievement, 110
    technology and, 110–11
    21st century skills and, 111
educational institutions, 97. *See also*
    higher education; pedagogy
EDUCAUSE, 157
Ehrlich, T., 7

eLearning Commons (eLC), 131
Elliott, S. N., 83
Encyclopedia Britannica, 154
EOTO. *See* Each One, Teach One
ePortfolios, 49
eService-Learning. *See also* Hybrid
    I eService-Learning; Hybrid II
    eService-Learning; Hybrid III
    eService-Learning; service-learning
in action, 21–22
affective learning from, 101
applications, 23
assessment tools, 45
barriers to, 20
benefits of, 23
case for, 17–18
clear linkage in, 24
communication, 64
community partners, 47
connective learning from, 101
content delivery, 63
core components of, 23, 24
course creation, 46–51, 53
course formats, 43
course outcomes, 46
defined, 41
direct format, 43
emerging, 26, 72, 110
essential steps, 53
evaluation in, 24
extreme, 25, 31–32, 36
format designing, 42–43
forms of, 43
fundamentals of, 20–21
future applications of, 164–66
incorporation of, into online courses,
    33–35
incremental approach to, 34
indirect format, 43
institutionalizing, 35–36
integration of, 20–21
IS/IT curriculum and, 96
learning connection in, 23
marketing, 47

Missouri State University
experiences, 77
Missouri State University
implementation of, 74–75
Missouri State University model
for, 73
Missouri State University program
for, 71–72
new assessment efforts, 82
newsletter, 36
nonprofit organizations and, 96–99
optional, 79–80
participant demographics, 79–80
post-course survey questions, 80
practical advice for, 34
preparation in, 24
Proposal, 76
reflection in, 23, 78–79
service delivery, 63–64
service in, 24
service-learning compared with,
29–32
service-learning conversion to, 32–33
social media, 47
structured reflection in, 24
students and, 100
syllabus, 46–51, 53
technology and, 62–65
technology utilized with, 76–77
training, 35–36
21st century skills and, 29–31
types of, 25–28
Waldner, McGorry, and Widener on,
41, 72–73
web design courses and, 93
ethical leadership, 70
evaluation
in eService-Learning, 24
in service-learning, 13
experiential learning, 90–92
Extreme eService-Learning, 25
Burton on, 122
classes, 36
client commitment in, 125–26

client meeting in, 125
client relationships in, 127
course content, 121–22
course development, 123–24
course tools, 121–22
defined, 120
electronic resources, 126
essential tools, 126
instructor availability, 126
at LaSalle University, 124–25
lessons from, 125–27
librarian meeting in, 126
limitations, 127–28
McGorry on, 121–22
online teamwork, 127–28
partner logistics, 122
performance of, 31–32
reflection, 126–27
sense of community in, 128
student availability, 121
time frame, 121
Eyler, J. S., 22, 128

Facebook, 111, 154
face-to-face service-learning, 135–38
Faculty Centers for Teaching and
Learning, 48
Faculty Focus, 41
Faculty Senate, 48
Faculty Survey of Course
Objectives, 45
First-Year Experience, 71–72, 76
service-learning for, 73
*Five High-Impact Practices: Research on
Learning Outcomes, Completion,
and Quality*, 15
focus groups, 45
Fottler, M. D., 122
Free Learning (Downes), 160–61

GEP 101, 71–72
Giles, D. E., 22, 128
Global Citizen, 47
Goldring, E., 83

Google Docs, 65
Google Maps, 153
Google Moderator, 157
Gray, C. J., 22
Green, F. P., 27
Groban, Josh, 159–60
Guatemala, 27, 122

Hamby, E. F., 124
Hamerlinck, John, 2
Hamline University, 28, 60
    civic awareness at, 111
    student interviews, 111–16
health organizations, 97
Hicks, Delores, 107–08
higher education
    connectivism in, 155–57
    costs of, 150
    creativity in, 159–60
    difficulties in, 150–52
    openness in, 160–61
    opportunities, 161–62
    personal learning network and,
        157–59
    social media and, 156
    student debt and, 150
    student success, 150
    technology and, 154–61
    in United States, 150–51
Higher Learning Commission, 79
high-impact educational practices
AAC&U on, 16
defined, 14–15
service-learning and, 15–17
*High-Impact Educational Practices:
    What They Are, Who Has Access
    to Them, and Why They
    Matter*, 14
high-quality service, 13
Hill, Christopher, 41
Hilton, Denny, 108, 153
HR, 32–33
HTML, 91
Hurricane Andrew, 117

Hurricane Katrina, 105–6, 112, 117
Hybrid I eService-Learning, 73–74
    benefits of, 85
    defined, 26–27
    Hybrid III compared with, 135–42
    qualitative analysis of, 132
    at UGA, 132
    Waldner on, 139
Hybrid II eService-Learning, 89–90
    Blackboard in, 92
    civic engagement in, 95–96
    community partners in, 102–4
    course content in, 95–96
    course development, 92
    critical success factors for, 104–5
    defined, 27–28
    design of, 102–4
    model, 90
    off-line components of, 94
    online components of, 92–94
    students in, 99–102
Hybrid III eService-Learning
    in Avalon High School,
        106–107
    defined, 28, 108
    Depot House, 108
    Hybrid I compared with, 135–41
    Martin Luther King Science and
        Technology Magnet
        School, 107
    at UGA, 135–38
    Waldner on, 139

Ibuka, Masaru, 160
ICT. *See* information,
    communications,
    and technology
IdeaScale, 157
indirect service-learning, 11–12
information, communications, and
    technology (ICT), 29
information skills, 29
innovation skills, 29
institutionalization, 35–36

Institutional Self-Assessment Tool for
    Service-Learning Sustainability
    Rubric, 84
instructors
    availability of, 126
    relationships with, 136
integrated learning, 13
Integrated Service-Learning (ISL), 75
internships, 11
interviews. *See* student interviews
ipadio, 154
IS/IT curriculum, 95–96
    course content, 95
    eService-Learning and, 96
    goals of, 96
ISL. *See* Integrated Service-Learning

Johnston, Shameka, 21, 30
Jonassen, D. H., 59–60

Korea, 159–60
Kuh, George, 14

LaSalle University, 124–25
Lazar, J., 27
leadership, 114
learning
    academic, 145
    affective, 101
    civic, 8
    connective, 101, 102
    experiential, 90
    fostering, 59–60
    integrated, 13
    longer term outcomes, 103
    National Task Force on Civic
        Learning and Democratic
        Engagement framework for, 9
    online, 21, 131
    skills, 29
    with technology, 58–59
    at UGA, 134–35
learning management system
    (LMS), 76

Levesque, Chantal, 80
liability, 54
liberal arts, 123
librarians, 122
libraries, 98
    databases, 122
life skills, 29–30
Likert scale, 80, 82
LMS. *See* learning management system
Lumen Learning, 151

MacArthur Foundation, 161
Madam Julia's, 109
Malvey, D. M., 25, 124
mapping, 155
Martin Luther King Science and
        Technology Magnet
        School, 108
    Hybrid III eService-Learning
        at, 108
massive open online courses (MOOCs),
        158, 161
Mazur, Eric, 152
McGorry, Sue, 1, 25, 108
    on eService-Learning definition, 41
    on eService-Learning
        models, 72–73
    on Extreme eService-Learning,
        121–22
media literacy skills, 29
Mihalynuk, T. V., 62
Miller-Keys University, 21
Miner Lite, 64–65
Missouri Department of Higher
        Education, 48
    CASL core elements, 51
Missouri General Assembly, 69
Missouri State University, 49–50
    CASL office, 82–85
    critical thinking, 87
    data collection, 79–80
    eService-Learning experiences in, 77
    eService-Learning implementation,
        74–75

eService-Learning model, 73
eService-Learning program, 71–72
Mission Statement, 69–70
Office of Assessment, 82
Office of Citizenship and Service-
Learning, 51
public affairs mission, 70, 88
service-learning in, 44
mixed hybrid eService-Learning, 130
discussion of, 139–41
at UGA, 131–32
MOOCs. *See* massive open online
courses
moral reasoning, 144
Mosley, P. H., 27
Murphy, J., 83

NASA, 58
National Center for Education
Statistics, 74
National Task Force on Civic Learning
and Democratic Engagement, 8
framework for learning from, 9
National Youth Leadership Council, 10
NCA Division I, 69
New Orleans, 105–6
nonprofit organizations, 92
eService-Learning and, 96–99
Nordyke, Katherine, 2, 26
Now You See It (Davidson), 151–52,
165–66
nursing homes, 98

ODK. *See* Open Data Kit
Office of Citizenship, 70–71
online community
development of, 60–61
service-learning outcomes
and, 136
online components
feedback in, 95
of Hybrid II eService-Learning,
92, 94
interaction in, 92, 94

online courses, 33–35
massive open, 158, 161
Waldner on, 42
online learning, 21, 131
online teachers, 17
online teamwork, 127–28
Open Data Kit (ODK), 64
Open Education Week, 160

Pace University, 99, 100
service-learning at, 90
partners. *See* community partners
pedagogy
civic engagement and, 9–10
of community engagement, 11
Peer Instruction (Mazur), 152
personal growth, 99–100
personal learning network (PLN),
157–59
personal skills development, 144
Pew Internet, 152
photo release, 55
Photoshop, 91
plagiarism, 49
PLN. *See* personal learning network
podcasting, 65
Porter, A., 83
post-traumatic stress disorder (PTSD),
107, 112, 117
PowerPoint, 49, 78
Pratt, David, 41
Preece, J., 27
Prentice, M., 45
President's Higher Education
Community Service Honor
Roll, 131
President's Honor Roll, 79
problem based service-learning, 91
professional skills development, 144
PTSD. *See* post-traumatic stress
disorder
Public Affairs Conference, 70
Public Affairs Scale, 80
results, 80–81

Public Affairs Week, 70
publication permission, 55
Purdue University, 41

Quantitative Data Analysis (QDA),
    64–65

reflection
    in eService-Learning, 23, 78–79
    Extreme eService-learning, 126–27
    in service-learning, 13, 136
    structured, 24
    technology and, 65
Registrar's Office, 56
research-based service-learning, 12
Roberts, K., 122
Robinson, G., 45

Saltmarsh, J., 7
Scoop.it, 153–54
SeeClickFix, 153
Seifer, S. D., 62
SELEB. *See* Service-Learning Benefit
    scale
self-knowledge, 99–101
Seniorcorp, 165
service delivery, 63–64
service-learning
    advocacy, 12
    Ash and Clayton on, 41
    benefits of, 22–23
    civic-based, 91
    civic responsibility in, 13
    collaboration, 13
    consulting-based, 91
    continuum of, 25
    core element checklist, 57
    course requirements, 75–76
    course statement, 56
    defined, 10–12
    direct, 11
    elements of, 13–14
    eService-Learning compared with,
        29–32

eService-Learning conversion
    from, 32–33
    evaluation in, 13
    experience, 44–45
    face-to-face, 135–38
    for First-Year Experience, 73
    forms of, 43
    high-impact educational practices
        and, 15–17
    high-quality service in, 13
    indirect, 11–12
    instructor relationship in, 136
    integrated learning in, 13
    in Missouri State University, 44
    online discussion and, 136
    in online environment, 41–51
    online learning and, 21
    for online teachers, 17
    outcomes, 136
    at Pace University, 90
    paragraph, 56
    problem-based, 91
    reflection in, 13, 136
    research-based, 12
    skill development, 18
    student voice in, 13
    tasks, 62
    technology-based courses, 95–96
    technology in, 61–62
Service-Learning Benefit (SELEB)
    scale, 133
Service Oriented Field
    Experience, 28
shelters, 98
Shirky, Clay, 154, 159
Siemens, George, 156, 161
Skype, 32–33, 34
Sloan Consortium, 72
Smith-Robbins, Sarah, 156
social media, 159
    eService-Learning and, 47
    higher education and, 156
social services, 98
special interests groups, 98

special needs children, 50
St. Charles Guest House, 108
Stenson, C. M., 22
Storify, 154
St. Paul, 106
Strait, Jean, 2, 28, 106
structured reflection, 24
student interviews, 111–16
  career in, 115
  communication in, 113, 115
  discussion of, 116
  fears in, 113
  leadership in, 114, 115
  participant demographics, 111
  questions, 111–12
  theme analysis, 112
  year 1 and year 2 responses, 113–14
  year 3 and year 4 responses,
    114–16
students
  academic achievement of, 109
  debt of, 150
  eService-Learning and, 100
  Extreme eService-Learning, 121
  in Hybrid II eService-Learning,
    99–102
  personal growth of, 99, 101
  self-knowledge of, 99, 101
  success of, 150
  voice, 13
Student Survey of Course
    Objectives, 45
Sullivan, B., 122
surveys, 45
  instruments, 133
  participants, 134
  post-course, 80

teach-back, 33–34
technology
  communication and, 64
  community engagement and,
    154–61
  content delivery, 63

for data collection and analysis,
    64–65
  EOTO and, 110–11
  eService-Learning and, 62–65
  eService-Learning courses utilizing,
    76–77
  examples of uses, 62
  higher education and, 154–61
  instructional impact, 60
  knowledge construction and, 59–60
  learning with, 58–59
  online community and, 60–61
  reflection and, 65
  service delivery, 63–64
  in service-learning courses, 95–96
  teaching, 61
  tools, 62–65
  21st century skills and, 152
  virtual culture and, 60–61
Themeefly, 153–54
Thrive Appalachia, 21
transactional courses, 26
transformational courses, 26
transgender community, 153
21st century skills
  EOTO and, 111
  eService-Learning and, 29–31
  technology and, 154
Twitter, 112, 154

United States, higher education in,
    150–51
University of Georgia (UGA)
  Hybrid I eService-Learning at, 132
  Hybrid III eService-Learning at,
    135–38
  learning outcomes at, 134–35
  mixed hybrid eService-Learning in,
    131–32
  Office of Online Learning, 131
  Office of Service-Learning, 131–32
  survey instruments, 133
  survey participants, 133–34
  variables and analyses, 134–38

Vanderbilt Assessment of Leadership in
    Education, 83
virtual culture, 60–61
volunteerism, 11

Waldner, Leora, 1, 2, 108, 122, 131–32
    on eService-Learning definition, 41
    on eService-Learning models, 72–73
    on Hybrid I and Hybrid III, 139
    on online courses, 42
web design, 91–94
    courses, 93
    eService-Learning and, 93

Weinberger, David, 157
Widener, M. C., 108, 122
    on eService-Learning definition, 41
    on eService-Learning models,
        72–73
Wikipedia, 154, 159
Wiley, David, 151, 155, 160
William H. Darr School of
    Agriculture, 69

youth services, 98
YouTube, 49, 79, 154

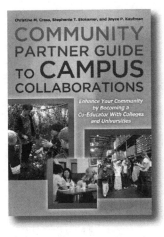

Community Partner Guide to Campus Collaborations

Strategies for Enhancing Your Community as a Co-Educator
Christine M. Cress, Stephanie T. Stokamer, and Joyce P. Kaufman

"Interacting with colleges can be confusing and frustrating. We learned the hard way through trial and error over the years. This book has great strategies for developing effective collaborations from the outset so that resources are leveraged for education and improvement."

—Sheila, Boys and Girls Club

"VERY strong and well-written chapters with lots of gold that I think community organizations will find very helpful."

—Melia, Hands on Greater Portland

"The format and visual cues make the Guide easy to scan for quick tips and ideas. Also, the information is comprehensive regarding research-based practices, but the writing is friendly and engaging for all non-profit sectors and community agencies. Lots of practical examples."

—Juan, Immigrant Empowerment

This guide offers insights and strategies to leverage student learning and community empowerment for the benefit of both community partners and educational institutions. Recognizing both the possibilities and the pitfalls of community-campus collaborations, it demystifies the often confusing terminology of education, explains how to locate the right individuals on campus, and addresses issues of mission, expectations for roles, tasks, training, supervision, and evaluation that can be fraught with miscommunication and misunderstanding.

Most importantly it provides a model for achieving full reciprocity in what can be an unbalanced relationship between community and campus partners so that all stakeholders can derive the maximum benefit from their collaboration.

It is available in sets of six or twelve, at reduced prices, to facilitate its use for planning, and for training of leaders engaged in partnerships.

Sty/us

22883 Quicksilver Drive
Sterling, VA 20166-2102

Subscribe to our e-mail alerts: www.Styluspub.com

Also available from Stylus

Learning through Serving
A Student Guidebook for Service-Learning and Civic Engagement Across Academic Disciplines and Cultural Communities
Second Edition
Christine M. Cress, Peter J. Collier, Vicki L. Reitenauer, and Associates

REVIEWS OF THE FIRST EDITION

"[This] is a self-directed guide for college students engaged in service-learning. The purpose of the book is to walk the reader through elements of learning and serving by focusing on how students can 'best provide meaningful service to a community agency or organization while simultaneously gaining new skills, knowledge, and understanding as an integrated aspect of the [student's] academic program.' [The authors] bring their expertise to the pages of this helpful and practical guide for college students engaged in service-learning. Intended as a textbook, this work reads like a conversation between the authors and the college student learner. The publication is student-friendly, comprehensive, easy to follow, and full of helpful activities."

—Journal of College Student Development

"Finally, a companion reader for students in service-learning courses! It is filled with meaningful exercises to help students make sense of their service experience and relate it to the course content. This is an important contribution to the field of service learning and faculty should utilize this book to help students understand and make the most of their service-learning experience."

—Elaine K. Ikeda, Executive Director, California Campus Compact

This text is a student-friendly, self-directed guide to service-learning that:

- Develops the skills needed to succeed
- Clearly links service-learning to the learning goals of the course
- Combines self-study and peer-study workbook formats with
- ctivities that can be incorporated in class, to give teachers maximum flexibility in structuring their service-learning courses
- Promotes independent and collaborative learning
- Equally suitable for courses of a few weeks' or a few months' duration
- Shows students how to assess progress and communicate end-results
- Is written for students participating in service learning as a class, but also suitable for students working individually on a project